MANAGING HUMAN RESOURCES
IN
SCHOOLS AND COLLEGES

Other titles in the University of Leicester MBA Series

Managing human resources
in
schools and colleges

John O'Neill, David Middlewood and Derek Glover

University of Leicester
EMDU

MBA in educational management by distance learning

Core Unit 3

LONGMAN

MANAGING HUMAN RESOURCES IN SCHOOLS AND COLLEGES

Published by Longman Information and Reference, Longman Group Limited, 6th floor, Westgate House, The High, Harlow, Essex CM20 1YR, England and Associated Companies throughout the world.

A catalogue record for this book is available from The British Library

ISBN 0-582-24570-2

Index prepared by Christopher Bowring-Carr
Typeset by Jeremy Spencer
Printed by Page Bros, Norwich

Contents

Contributors

John O'Neill lectures in educational management with the Educational Management Development Unit. He spent ten years teaching students with SEN in mainstream and special education. John's research interests include middle management development and inter-school collaboration.

David Middlewood is Senior Tutor with the Educational Management Development Unit. His special responsibility is for courses in Management Development and Training, which are based in schools or colleges. He spent over twenty years teaching in schools, including nine years as a headteacher. His special interests include teachers' career development, appraisal, staff development and management structures.

Derek Glover (Consultant) was, for eighteen years, head of Burford School, Oxfordshire. This was a complex organization with boarding, agricultural and community units. As a result he became interested in aspects of management theory. He took early retirement in order to complete his PhD with the Open University and to join the successful schools' centre at Keele University. He now works part-time for both those universities and the EMDU at Leicester. His particular interests are in finance and external relations.

1. Introduction

This is the core study unit for the *Human Resource Management in Education* module.

Study focus

The purposes of the unit are to:

- introduce the principal theoretical and ethical issues which underpin approaches to the management of staff in schools and colleges;
- examine a range of management frameworks for the application of theory into practice in human resource management; and
- link the theory and practice of human resource management to the autonomous school and college context of the 1990s.

We hope that by the end of this unit you will have:

- **developed** an informed and critical overview of the major areas of theory;
- **reflected** on and articulated your own and your institution's values;
- **examined** your own and your institution's current practice;
- **explored** alternative approaches to current practice;
- **clarified** the linkages between theory, values and management strategy in your own school or college situation.

You may also have your own, more specific, objectives for this unit which you want to list at this stage.

-
-
-

Activities

In this unit we use a range of activities which ask you to:

- **analyse** and **reflect** on what you have read;
- use what you have read to help **examine** your own practice;
- constructively **criticize** your and your institution's practice.

The activities serve different functions; the letter or letters in brackets in the heading of each activity indicate the following:

- reflection (R);
- application (A); and
- conceptualization (C).

Some activities are based on readings from the core text which has been written to accompany the course:

> Bush, T. and West-Burnham, J. (eds) (1994) *The Principles of Educational Management*,
> Harlow: Longman.

Other activities focus on your experience, and some require further investigation which will introduce you to research methods which you might use in later work. Within the range of activities some will be more relevant to your own needs and interests. We expect that you might choose to spend more time on some activities than others, or indeed, to link appropriate activities into the design of your assignment for this module.

Structure of the unit

As you can see from the contents page, the unit is divided into two halves:

PART I   MANAGEMENT ISSUES
PART II   MANAGEMENT APPLICATIONS

Each half comprises several sections. All the sections are similar in that they contain:

- an introduction which sets out the purpose and study focus for the section;
- a synthesis of theoretical perspectives;
- an examination of management implications;
- a range of activities; and
- a summary of key learning points.

We have written the unit's sections in a certain order which you may wish to follow in sequence, as presented. Equally, we acknowledge that, particularly with more experienced students, you may wish to organize your study in a different way, according to your own working priorities, personal preferences or interests, and learning needs. You may wish, for example, to study:

- **'Individual and organizational development'** and **'Induction and mentoring'** together; or
- **'People or performance?'** together with **'Induction and mentoring'**.

We have attempted to structure the unit almost as a set of self-contained study sections of manageable length, so as to accommodate this sort of approach to your study. We hope that you will feel comfortable with the notion of revisiting certain sections within the unit in order to apply recurring **issues** to different management **applications**. We would, however, suggest that you read this section thoroughly **before** you decide in order to familiarize yourself with the content, rationale and structure of the unit.

Your study of HRM

We feel it is important to approach the study of staff management aware of the fact that it is neither value neutral in **interpretation** nor can it be completely rational in **implementation**. We explain this distinction below.

❑ Interpretation

The way the curriculum is structured in your school or college reflects certain judgements and decisions about the purpose of educational organizations, the role of teachers and the status of students. Decisions will have been made about the appropriate level of funding for certain age groups of students, the best way to resource courses and how to measure attainment. The level of involvement of parents, governors and the wider community will vary considerably even between two neighbouring institutions which serve similar catchment areas.

The differences in curriculum, organization, staffing, internal and external relations all reflect underlying values about the best way to 'manage' formal education.

It is the same with the study of HRM. Your, and your institution's, preferred approach to the management of staff is informed by values which are reflected in HRM policy and practice. Thus, in this unit, the part focusing on MANAGEMENT ISSUES is concerned with the philosophical, ethical and ideological aspects of HRM in education. It links HRM approaches to differences in values and perceptions about what the management of staff is intended to achieve in educational organizations, and how those values might be expressed in terms of:

- strategy;
- policy; and
- operational procedures.

The differences between apparently similar schools and colleges are manifold. Nuances of approach and organization, management style, organizational culture ('the way we do things around here') are reflected in the discussions contained in MANAGEMENT ISSUES .

An exploration of your own values and norms as a manager creates an agenda in terms of the principles which you want to inform your approach to the management of staff in your particular institution. That, of course, still begs the question of how to put those principles into practice, and how to do so in the context of constraints and opportunities which exist within your own school or college.

❑ Implementation

The HRM literature, in education and elsewhere, now reflects a host of prescriptions about what to do in order to get the best out of people. Our approach in this unit is somewhat different because we ask you to:

- analyse your own and your institution's **value** stance in management **issues**; and only then,
- apply those values and principles to practical **applications** in school or college.

The part focusing on MANAGEMENT APPLICATIONS, then, attempts to bridge the gap between principle and practice by identifying frameworks which act as tangible tools for translating principle into coherent and informed practice. In the APPLICATIONS half of the unit we focus on recruitment, selection, induction and mentoring and appraisal.

Human resource management ISSUES and APPLICATIONS are symbiotic: management is an essentially practical, and ultimately very pragmatic, activity; hence principle informs practice. Successful practice reinforces those principles whereas lack of success tends to lead to the questioning of underlying principles, at both organizational and individual manager level.

We feel that the unit as a whole offers an informed approach to HRM in autonomous schools and colleges in that:

- it advocates the development of guiding principles based on values;
- it translates principles into frameworks for practice;
- it informs management practice with themes related to the actual educational context of the 1990s; and
- it gives pre-eminence to the relationship between the management of staff and enhanced learning experiences for students.

The importance of HRM in education

As you work through this text you will become increasingly aware of our basic argument for the unit as a whole which is that effective human resource management (HRM) is the key to the provision of high quality educational experiences. The term itself, human resource management, may still appear problematic, perhaps even slightly distasteful, in education where concepts of professionalism, professional autonomy and collegial approaches to decision-making militate against the perception of teachers as a resource to be managed, manipulated or directed in pursuit of school or college objectives. We, however, do not see HRM approaches and professionalism as mutually incompatible. Indeed, we base our assertion on an apparently simple *premise* which we believe would have the support of professional colleagues in schools or colleges.

> Educational organizations depend for their success on the **quality**, **commitment** and **performance** of the **people** who work there.

The content of this unit is then, in essence, an exploration of the four key terms which make up that premise. In order to introduce you to the values which underpin **our** understanding of HRM in education we 'unpack' each of our key terms below.

Quality

The quality of staff in educational organizations is an issue of both **specification** and **development.** Informed recruitment and selection procedures are an essential element of specification: what job needs to be done and what sort of person do we need to carry out that job? Quality is, however, about much more than appointing the most suitable candidate.

Drucker (1988) argues that people as a basic resource are unique in the sense that the quality of their performance is dependent on a host of organizational variables. Drucker implies that effective organizations are fully aware of the fact that the management support they provide makes a direct and qualitative difference to the level of performance of individual staff and the contribution they make to the work of the institution.

Activity 1.1 (R)

Recall for a moment your appointment to your present post. Focus on your feelings of:

- self-confidence
- ability to do the job
- awareness of other people's expectations of you

How did you feel the week before you started? on your first day? at the end of your first term?

Our comments

We imagine that your feelings of increasing confidence and competence in your present post are attributable in no small measure to your personal and professional qualities and skills but also, in great part, to the support and encouragement which have been provided for you by others within your teaching team, department or institution. Unfortunately, in some instances, the situation may be very different; you, or colleagues or friends, will have experience of working in institutions, or with groups of people, where support and encouragement are not forthcoming; where the prevailing culture is one of 'sink or swim' or learning in the 'school of hard knocks'. Whatever the quality of your own treatment, you will know from your own experience that your professional effectiveness is contingent upon support from others. Effective schools and colleges display a similar awareness and actively manage the levels of support they provide for staff so that the quality of staff contributions increases rather than decreases with time.

Commitment

Wanting to do well, to feel a sense of belonging to a group or team of people working towards the same goals and being determined to achieve those goals or targets are natural aspirations for staff in any organization. Indeed, conscientious classroom teachers constantly attempt to develop those same qualities amongst students with whom they work.

From an HRM perspective, commitment is something that has to be managed; it cannot be assumed. Developing commitment is about:

- **articulating** a clear sense of purpose, so that staff know what they are supposed to be doing and why;
- **translating** a sense of purpose into clear and realistic objectives for the institution, groups and individuals;
- **removing** barriers to and **providing** opportunities for the achievement of those objectives;
- **involving** staff in developing that sense of purpose and identifying targets so that, whenever possible, they feel ownership of their work;
- **integrating** staff within the work of the school or college so that they feel their contribution is essential and unique; and
- visibly **valuing** staff and the qualities, skills and expertise they bring to the organization.

Effective schools and colleges do not assume that an offer of employment is sufficient to secure commitment but, rather, that gaining commitment involves active encouragement, support and open communication. Various writers (e.g. Beare et al., 1989; Caldwell and Spinks, 1992; West-Burnham, 1992; Fullan and Hargreaves, 1992; Murgatroyd and Morgan, 1993) emphasize the active role that needs to be taken by senior managers in organizations in:

- **articulating** organizational values and mission;
- **publicizing** acceptable performance standards;
- **involving** staff in decision-making;
- **bringing together** individuals and groups of staff to reinforce common objectives,

so that collective commitment to agreed organizational goals can be optimized.

Performance

As we suggest above, quality of performance is not an absolute standard. Performance differs between institutions and individuals according to a host of variables. Performance standards may be defined **for**, **with** or **by** individuals. Performance standards may seek to measure **input**, **process** or **outcome** factors or a combination of the three. They may be **qualitative** or **quantitative** in nature. Often the performance of individuals will depend on contributions from others within the immediate work group.

Traditionally the quality of individual student learning experiences has eluded satisfactory, objective definition. For some institutions ensuring regular attendance and developing basic levels of literacy, numeracy and social skills amongst students constitutes a meaningful and worthwhile set of objectives. For other institutions successful performance may only be measured against a benchmark of acceptable public examination results. For yet others, gaining and sustaining regular eye contact may be the realization of several years' effort on the part of student, teacher, therapist, parent and carer.

Just as the assessment of student attainment is complex, problematic and dependent on context, so it is with the performance of adults employed within educational organizations. The common elements between the two perspectives, however, are:

- the notion of promoting continuous progress and improvement; and
- the provision of support and feedback on performance.

In order to perform at an optimum level adults need:

- **targets** against which they can measure progress;
- constructive **feedback** so that impressionistic and potentially subjective observations or assessments of performance are avoided;
- **reassurance** that mistakes are an inevitable and necessary part of both learning and higher levels of attainment;
- **structured support** so that difficulties can be addressed as they occur and resources provided to support further development; and
- frequent **recognition** of their achievements and contribution to the success of the school or college.

Observers of effective management practice in non-education sectors (e.g. Handy, 1987; Drucker, 1988) have consistently highlighted the need for organizations to view mistakes positively, as an inevitable by-product of striving for higher standards of performance. This is perhaps a difficult new paradigm for educationists to understand and adopt in a profession where the majority of practitioners have, historically, operated in classroom isolation, and where direct observation of performance has been the exception rather than the norm. In England and Wales the teaching profession's perceived ambivalence towards the introduction of a variety of mechanisms for increased professional accountability exemplifies the difficulties associated with direct assessment of individual and whole-school or college performance (Bush, 1994; West-Burnham, 1994a).

People

It is sometimes assumed that the term 'people in educational organizations' means **teachers**; not other adults working within the school or college, nor even the students for whose development and learning the institution, in theory, is established. Our understanding of this issue is clear:

1. The management of human resources in education focuses on **all** adults employed within the school or college and, in the case of external agencies and contractors, those who provide a service to the organization.

2. Although the management of students is not directly our concern in this unit, it is worth noting that many of the **principles** which apply to the effective management of staff, apply also to the management of the relationship between teacher and student.

3. The complexities associated with the management of learning in schools and colleges in the 1990s lead us firmly towards the conviction that HRM perspectives need to acknowledge the invaluable contributions made by all categories of staff to the work of the institution. As such we reject the historical iconography of the teacher as sole **provider** of support for student learning, as sole **arbiter** of what takes place within the classroom and as sole **worker** in the preparation, delivery and administration of all activities associated with the provision and assessment of teaching and learning. It is, perhaps, only with the introduction of financial autonomy at school and college level that institutions have begun to fully debate the merits of a more considered mix of teachers, other

professionals and ancillary staff at various levels within the establishment (NCE, 1993; O'Neill, 1994a; Mortimore et al., 1994).

The expectation that teachers alone should be the focus of human resource management in schools and colleges presents three significant difficulties for us:

1. It reinforces the historical notion that teachers can and should do everything, rather than concentrate on their most important professional role-responsibility as managers of the learning process;

2. It focuses on the teacher rather than the tasks which need to be done in terms of managing and supporting student learning; and

3. It fails to recognize other adults as significant and valuable members of teams which are structured to manage and support the learning process in a variety of ways.

An initial model for HRM in education

An HRM perspective which acknowledges the potential contributions of all adults employed within the institution has many benefits, not least because, for us, it incorporates each of the key terms in our original premise.

A broader definition of the term **people** is inclusive rather than exclusive. It suggests that each adult employed within the school or college plays a critical role in its success. Acknowledging the unique contribution of individuals engenders **commitment**. Equally it focuses managerial attention on the **quality** of people needed and how those people can most effectively be encouraged and empowered to work together as part of an effective team. The sharing of work amongst team members is informed by an analysis of which tasks need to be done. In turn, support for team members and their work suggests that clear objectives need to be established and agreed, against which **performance** can be monitored, measured and evaluated.

Your study of HRM in educational organizations

The idealistic, rational approach to the management of staff which we have just outlined may appear very remote from your own managerial experience in school or college. Before we proceed further, it may be a useful exercise for you to reflect on your own experience of being 'managed' in school or college and, if appropriate, your experience of managing other adults.

Activity 1.2 (A)

How would you characterize the way other people manage you in school or college?

What are your positive experiences of being managed by others?

What are your negative experiences of being managed by others?

What are your feelings about our **premise**, outlined above, for the module?

What are your feelings about our **model**, outlined above, for HRM in schools and colleges?

As a manager, what characterizes the way you manage other staff?

Our comments

The way you manage others is likely to be informed by your own experience of being managed. These experiences may be positive or negative. You may be fortunate to work with colleagues whose management style provides a positive role model and which you would like to emulate. Equally, you may have had negative experiences to date and be determined to manage others differently so that they do not suffer in the way that you feel you have done! Whatever your experiences to date we hope that your study of this unit will enable you to reflect on your previous and current practice and inform any strategies you adopt and action you take in the future.

◉ Reading 1

John O'Neill *Managing Human Resources* Chapter 10.

Please now read the first part of this chapter, up to but not including the section headed 'Strategic HRM'. As you read consider the ways in which your school or college recognizes the need to balance individual and institutional needs. Please do not consider our comments until you have completed the reading.

Our comments

Practice varies from organization to organization. It is likely, however, that you will have identified the importance of:

- commonly agreed and shared values within the working community;
- the imperative to make the most efficient use of scarce resources; and
- management processes which enable personal and institutional objectives to be balanced.

Part I Management issues

2. The meaning of HRM

Introduction

Human resource management is generally agreed to have emerged into common usage within management vocabularies during the 1980s. There is still some difference of opinion regarding the acceptability of HRM as a generic term for the management and development of staff within organizations. This section explores the differences between the two terms HRM and Personnel Management. We examine the reasons for the emergence of HRM as an apparently distinctive approach to the management of staff in organizations. We also consider arguments from sources which articulate a certain scepticism about the actual contribution of HRM to organizational effectiveness.

Study focus

At the end of this section you should be able to:

- distinguish between the major features of HRM and Personnel Management approaches;
- summarize the main strengths of an HRM approach to staff management;
- summarize the perceived limitations of HRM in practice.

Origins of HRM

The term Human Resource Management (HRM) began to appear regularly in mainstream management terminology during the 1980s (for a chronological overview see Armstrong, 1991; Beaumont, 1993; Goss, 1994). In essence the term is intended to offer a broader, strategic and more dynamic interpretation of the role of effective staff management in organizations than had been the norm in previous decades. Amongst proponents of HRM approaches, personnel management carries largely negative connotations.

Personnel management

Stereotypical (Guest, 1987) views of the distinction between the two approaches interpret personnel management as being concerned with the following:

- separating personnel function and workplace management;
- emphasizing administration, record-keeping and procedures;
- advocating procedural approaches to negotiation and conflict;
- being prescriptive rather than analytical in support of line managers;
- appearing reactive rather than proactive in response;
- promoting a reliance on personnel specialists.

From the above criteria we can see that personnel management is criticized because it appears removed from the immediate concerns of managers. It suggests that difficulties be dealt with via standardized procedural arrangements by specialists rather than line managers, and it emphasizes sanitized staff management administrative **procedures** at the expense of customized **processes** geared towards the active motivation and involvement of individuals within the workplace.

The move towards HRM approaches is attributable to the notion that traditional, specialist personnel provision:

- is unsustainably expensive in financial and human terms;
- is highly bureaucratic;
- leads to lengthy delay between identification of need and intervention;
- offers solutions which work in artificial or simulated situations but are difficult to apply in the workplace;
- threatens the relationship between line manager and subordinate; and
- is reliant on, and perpetuates the mystique of, the perceived expertise of personnel specialists rather than focusing on the development of line manager capability.

If this argument appears too remote from your immediate experience as an educationist, we can, perhaps, usefully apply the personnel management versus HRM debate to an analogous development in education: the management of special educational needs (SEN) provision in mainstream schools and colleges since 1978, when the Warnock Committee's report was published.

The period since the publication of that report has been characterized by a move in schools and colleges away from segregated provision in stand alone 'remedial' departments or classes towards the notion of 'learning support' which places the classroom teacher at the heart of any approach to the management of special educational needs. The SEN co-ordinator is seen increasingly as a **consultant** whose role is to support the basic relationship between learner and teacher, to offer **support and expertise** where appropriate and to suggest appropriate **strategies** rather than herself implement specific intervention programmes. The new relationship is based on three key premises:

- the co-ordinator supports both teacher and learner;
- the teacher's redefined role requires the development of higher order interpersonal and professional skills; and
- the teacher needs to be encouraged to actively 'access' the expertise of the co-ordinator as and when the teacher feels it necessary.

This redefined role relationship, then, emphasizes the central importance of the classroom teacher as manager of the learning situation. The teacher is encouraged to manage the relationship between herself and the student and also any intervention, using the SEN co-ordinator for advice and support. We feel that the parallels between this shift of responsibilities and that advocated by HRM proponents are clear.

In the same way that traditional personnel management contains similarities with historical approaches to SEN provision in schools and colleges, so the newly defined role and responsibilities of the SEN co-ordinator, or learning consultant, can be compared with HRM approaches in organizations.

The HRM 'approach' has been adopted with enthusiasm in many mainstream organizations. Its supporters argue that the approach offers significant benefits to organizations.

Human Resources Management

HRM approaches typically contain the following features. They:

- measure actions against the strategic objectives of the organization as a whole;
- emphasize the central importance of the line manager;
- advocate customized, individual responses to intervention;

- focus on positive motivation rather than negative control;
- use process rather than standardized procedures;
- are considered proactive rather than reactive;
- are fully integrated into the day-to-day management of the organization; and
- encourage purposeful negotiation and the resolution of potential conflict between manager and managed.

As with changing SEN 'consultant' or 'co-ordinator' models of approach in schools and colleges, HRM theory is predicated on the principles of concern for the quality of relationships, a desire to reduce unnecessary bureaucracy and a concern to see staff management issues as the routine preserve of the line manager, to be addressed in the workplace.

The rationale is summarized by Fowler (1988, p.1) who applies the HRM approach to a local government context:

- People are the primary resource.
- Personnel policies and practices need to be integrated with the total direction and management of the authority.
- Strategic planning, and a matching of the style of employment practice to the authority's culture, is necessary to maximize the effectiveness of the human resource.
- Human resource management is a prime responsibility of all managers, not a specialist role.

Activity 2.1 (R)

How is the deployment and development of staff structured within your school or college? Apply Fowler's points listed above to your situation and then produce a set of recommendations for change to enhance managerial effectiveness.

Our comments

You will, no doubt, have found some problems in applying the list to the way things are managed in your school or college. Overall though, you may well conclude that an approach which emphasizes the importance of line managers has advantages for autonomous schools and colleges. For example, it links staff management to the overall strategic direction of the institution and it reinforces the notion that the fundamentally important relationship between manager and managed should reflect the culture of the school or college.

Fowler's objectives appear logical and highly laudable but, as you might expect, the perceived gap between academic rhetoric and the reality of organizational practice has caused some writers to question the validity of HRM as a feasible, practicable approach to the management of staff, particularly in large and complex organizations. According to their critics HRM approaches have serious shortcomings. Armstrong (1991), Beaumont (1993) and Goss(1994) offer a useful synthesis of the main objections to HRM approaches, which we summarize below:

1. The distinction is one of simple, and irrelevant, nomenclature. The substantive issue is the choice between either a 'hard' approach, which views people as just another resource to be managed efficiently in order to meet organizational objectives; or a 'soft' approach, which emphasizes staff involvement, awareness and commitment in order to motivate staff to perform better than they otherwise would.

2. A focus on process and relationships marginalizes the bureaucratic, administrative infrastructure which is needed to manage necessarily standardized personnel procedures, often within a framework of statutory requirements or local 'custom and practice'.

3. There is limited empirical evidence which demonstrates that HRM specific approaches work in practice. As with 'learning support', the model is normative and experience, to date, fails to provide data in support of rhetorical exhortations by HRM advocates.

4. HRM approaches rely heavily on the commitment and active participation of line managers.

5. HRM approaches focus on individual rather than collective bargaining arrangements and, as such, offer little protection to traditionally disadvantaged or exploited sections of the workforce, in particular women (see, for example, Steele, 1992).

Nevertheless, despite these criticisms, the impetus for an increased focus on HRM approaches in the last decade or more demonstrates a high degree of similarity between the performance priorities of educational and other types of organization (Riches and Morgan, 1989), together with a growing realization that optimum, rather than merely adequate, levels of organizational performance depend on the effective management of human resources.

We examine the implications of the relationship between these increased performance priorities and HRM strategies, within an educational context, in the following section.

◉ Readings 2 and 3

John O'Neill *Managing Human Resources* Chapter 10.

Please now read the section of this chapter entitled 'Strategic HRM', and also from

Marianne Coleman *Women in Educational Management* Chapter 9.

the section headed 'Male and female 'styles' of management'. These two readings bring together the issues of HRM and gender. As you read consider the extent to which recognition of 'style' might affect approaches to HRM. Our comments are shown below but please do not read them until you have completed the activity.

Our comments

Some aspects of HRM can be interpreted as 'masculine' with their emphasis on performance related hard indicators. At the same time one can argue the need for the more 'feminine' management skills of persuasion, negotiation and positive encouragement. In short, effective management, especially in a people dominated environment, requires both.

Key learning points

- Personnel management approaches are perceived to emphasize administration and standardized responses to situations, and highlight the role of personnel specialists; HRM approaches advocate customized responses and highlight the importance of line managers.
- HRM approaches are considered highly normative; they emphasize staff motivation, commitment and involvement but there is limited empirical evidence to demonstrate their effectiveness in practice.
- Personnel management approaches rely on the credibility of personnel specialists; HRM approaches rely on the active participation of line managers.
- Personnel management approaches are seen as reactive and operationally oriented; HRM approaches are considered proactive and strategically oriented.
- HRM approaches provide a background against which the rapid and complex changes within education can be managed.

3. HRM in education

Introduction

In educational organizations the majority of personnel management functions have historically come within the remit of the local education authority (LEA) with the role of schools and colleges, until recently, being limited to the deployment of staffing establishments decided elsewhere. With the development of autonomous educational institutions the role of the institution has expanded rapidly in terms both of scope and complexity. Schools and colleges, however, face the additional challenge of coming to terms with the management implications of the HRM versus personnel management debate. In the further education (FE) sector, incorporation has meant that colleges, like grant-maintained (GM) schools, have full employer responsibilities and obligations (Warner and Crosthwaite, 1992). Within the maintained sector schools are faced with difficult decisions about which aspects of HRM administration and management can be managed well in-house and which need to be bought in as services from external agencies (Pryke, 1992).

Study focus

At the end of this section you should be able to:

- understand the strategic role of HRM in educational organizations;
- summarize the individual policy areas which institutions need to address;
- chronicle the changes in HRM practice initiated by the 1988 and subsequent education acts;
- examine the relevance of HRM approaches within different types and sizes of educational organization.

Changes in HRM in education

The increased focus on the contribution of staff to organizational success is reflected, in England and Wales, in specific central government initiatives, designed to enhance teaching and management performance in autonomous schools and colleges:

- a broadening of entry routes into the teaching profession;
- a strengthening of support arrangements for teachers at various career stages via
    - induction guidelines
    - mentoring schemes
    - attempts to develop taxonomies of professional and managerial competencies;
- the introduction of appraisal schemes;
- funding for professional development activities;
- the development of published performance indicators;
- a preference for links between pay and performance;
- an enhanced focus on the role played by non-teaching staff (NTS) (O'Neill 1994a, p.205).

These initiatives are of major significance for the education service in several ways. We examine their significance below.

1.   The pattern of entry, or re-entry, to the teaching profession in the 1990s is fragmenting. This suggests that schools and colleges will need to develop flexible management responses to cope with an increasingly diverse group of recruits whose previous work experiences, career aspirations and needs in terms of personal and professional support will all vary considerably. Research suggests that the following factors will be of particular significance:

- From the mid-1990s demographic changes suggest a reduction in the 'pool' of well-qualified graduates leading to increased competition for staff from other sectors (Buchan et al., 1988). However, in the United Kingdom the potential effects of such demographic 'downturns' are mitigated by factors such as the large increase in University entrance since 1988 and a fragile economic climate.
- Shortages of appropriately qualified teaching staff are likely to be subject-specific rather than across the board. Gilbert and van Haeften (1988) argue that 'supported self-study' and other, alternative, teaching and learning approaches are needed as practicable responses to teacher shortages.
- The numbers of qualified, but 'inactive', teachers are consistently identified (e.g. Buchan et al., 1988; NCE, 1993) as a potential, yet relatively untapped, source of supply:

   > Over 400,000 teachers are currently employed in the maintained sector in England and Wales. Part-time employment accounts for less than 5 per cent of the total. There are over 350,000 people with teaching qualifications currently not employed in the maintained sector, over half of whom (200,000) are female, aged 30–49 (Buchan et al., 1988, p.1).

2.   The introduction of institutionally based modes of Initial Teacher Training (ITT) implies that schools and colleges can seek to exercise more direct control over the style and type of initial training and the criteria which are used to select appropriate recruits at the point of entry to the profession. In the United States of America a model of 'professional practice schools' has been proposed (Levine, 1992) to train and induct entrants to the profession. The premise for a revised, school or college-based, approach to teacher-training is twofold:

- Traditional 'instructional' teaching methods are inappropriate responses to the management of pupil or student learning in the 1990s. The role of the teacher in autonomous schools and colleges, prompted jointly perhaps by developments in information technology and greatly increased curriculum complexity, is moving towards that of 'facilitator' rather than 'deliverer' of education (Handy and Aitken, 1986; Gilbert and van Haeften, 1988; Lofthouse, 1994).
- 'People tend to teach how they themselves have been taught' (Shanker 1992, p. vii). Hence, in order to prepare new, and returning, teachers for this unfamiliar 'facilitator' role, a new type of training institution is necessary, one in which preferred good practice is modelled and encouraged for, as Levine (1992, p.3) argues 'it is difficult to imagine significant change occurring in public education while the [...] education of teachers remains a mirror of the existing school model and a powerful way of reinforcing it.'

3.   Documented, perennial difficulties caused by teacher wastage (Buchan et al., 1988; NCE, 1993), particularly in urban and inner city areas, imply that initial recruitment is not the only staff management issue facing schools and colleges. The introduction of induction guidelines, mentoring schemes and teacher appraisal frameworks imply that historically weak levels of institutional support for staff contribute in a substantive way to inappropriately high levels of teacher turnover. In addition, in England and Wales, large-scale central government support for professional development activities since the early 1980s (see Williams, 1991) has indicated a recognition of the need to enable and encourage teachers to regularly update their professional skills and expertise in order to be able to deliver increasingly complex, externally prescribed curricula.

4.   Attempts to develop taxonomies of professional (DFE, 1993) and managerial (Earley, 1991) competences in education, and indeed to explicitly link pay and performance, reflect:

   a) the increased awareness in all types of organization of the importance of optimum employee involvement;

b) the need to identify appropriate standards of performance for individuals;

c) the importance of creating manageable agendas for individual employee development; and

d) recognition of the value of early identification of potential for promotion.

In service organizations, such as schools and colleges, the major area of expenditure is staff costs. It is in the organization's interests, therefore, to ensure value-for-money from staff and, by implication, prevent unnecessary wastage either via avoidable staff turnover or, just as significantly, from lack of motivation.

5.   A focus on staffing costs and levels of performance as major indicators of effective management within the organization suggests that schools and colleges need to be creative in terms of their approaches to staffing curricular activities, so that:

- professional teacher expertise, which is expensive and may be in short supply, is employed directly in the management of student learning; and
- administrative or support activities are delegated where appropriate to non-teaching staff who, in general, cost less.

This shift in perspective, from 'supply' to 'demand' led staffing (O'Neill, 1994a), is reflected in three tangible trends in schools and colleges. First, in the further education sector the use of large numbers of part-time staff (Fagg, 1991) suggests that teachers, in these instances, are employed specifically to staff certain, viable, curricular activities. Secondly, in the primary sector in particular there is, as yet largely anecdotal, evidence of schools using temporary salary incentives to support curriculum development; and, third, in both primary and secondary schools, budgetary autonomy has encouraged schools to more closely scrutinize the distinction between teaching and non-teaching roles (Mortimore et al., 1992). This has led to a broadening of the range and importance of activities undertaken by non-teaching staff, in both direct curriculum and more general managerial and administrative support (ibid.).

6.

The creation of an educational marketplace, via the ERA [Education Reform Act] and subsequent legislation, now has direct relevance for the recruitment of staff, just as much as students. With greater freedom to determine the range of benefits and working conditions on offer to individual staff, comes the realization that, particularly when seeking to attract quality staff, institutions are in direct competition with each other (O'Neill 1994a, p.207).

There are two important management issues for schools and colleges here which arise directly from the move towards autonomous schools and colleges:

a) As *de facto* employers of staff, schools and colleges can exercise much greater degrees of latitude in terms of pay and conditions of service. As Fagg (1991) indicates central government intention appears to be to urge employers, in the further and higher education sectors, to negotiate with staff on the basis of individual contracts wherever possible, leading eventually to the complete demise of collective bargaining and nationally determined norms.

b) However, schools and colleges have limited experience in technical and/or legal areas of personnel work, in the area of determining pay and conditions of service, or indeed, in the issues of performance related pay, discipline and grievance matters, welfare and equal opportunities. These issues, perceived as removed from the remit of managers in schools and colleges, have hitherto largely been resolved between professional associations and local or national government. Indeed, as Steele (1992) implies, collective bargaining arrangements at local government level have led to the establishment of more generous conditions of service for some groups of staff.

We give detailed consideration to how these issues might affect recruitment, selection and induction, for example, in the second half of the unit.

Activity 3.1 (A) (C) and 👁 **Reading 4**

Research method: interview
Arrange to interview the head or departmental head of your organization to ascertain how the environment for recruitment is changing. ***Please prepare your questions using the sections 'Teacher recruitment' and 'Teacher deployment' taken from:***

John O'Neill *Managing Human Resources* Chapter 10.

When you have completed the interview relate your findings to the six changes we have outlined above.

Our comments

The pace of change in the environment depends upon local conditions — the suburban or rural school, for example, is less likely to have problems in attracting staff. However, it may suffer from so much stability that the process of innovation and development may be hindered. Equally, any requirements for major retraining for existing staff may be a costly call on limited resources. These issues, however, are now part of the management brief of individual schools and colleges.

The gradual 'downloading' of more and more employer responsibilities to governing body level, and the transition of LEA services to a trading agency basis suggest that schools and colleges are now 'actively engaged across the full range of what are traditionally perceived as HRM or personnel functions' (O'Neill 1994a, p.206).

In this sense educational organizations, as autonomous institutions, need to develop highly customized HRM policies which reflect their own priorities in terms of recruiting, retaining and developing staff, rather than outdated national or local 'custom and practice' which belong to a period of LEA, as opposed to institutional, level of staff management.

Schools and colleges need to consider the following areas in developing their strategic approach to managing human resources:

Social responsibility — the philosophy of the organization toward the people it employs, covering areas such as equity, consideration of individual needs and fears, the quality of working life.

Employment — the level of personnel the organization wishes to employ, the provision of equal opportunity and reasonable security.

Pay — the level of pay and other benefits for employees and the extent to which pay systems are negotiated and disclosed.

Promotion — the attitude of the organization to providing long term career prospects and to promoting from within the organization.

Training — the scope of training and staff development schemes and the extent to which the organization proposes to subsidize education and training.

Industrial Relations — policies on union recognition, closed shops, the role of teacher representatives and shop stewards and the approach to dealing with grievances, discipline and redundancy (adapted from Armstrong 1984, p.22).

The key management issue which emerges for autonomous schools and colleges is the need to put in place policies for each of the above areas which reflect the aspirations, priorities and circumstances of the individual institution. These relate not only to the interpretation of statute in terms of employment law and equality of opportunity but also, and more significantly, to the broader ethical and social responsibility aspects of the employment and management of staff which distinguish one institution from another. Empirical evidence is limited in those areas of policy which were historically associated with national and local collective bargaining arrangements. The research conducted by Bush et al. (1993) suggests that GM schools have largely adopted existing LEA conditions of service agreements for staff. Changes, where they have taken place, have tended to be at the margins, and have proved largely beneficial for staff. By contrast, Elliott and Hall (1994) express serious reservations about the incorporation of further education colleges in terms of its detrimental effects on the pay and conditions of service of teaching staff. In our view, Armstrong's taxonomy provides a useful agenda for auditing both the spirit and the practice of human resource management policies within individual educational establishments.

Activity 3.2 (A) (R)

Consider the six functions listed above by Armstrong in relation to your institution. For each function note:

- Whether a policy exists?
- How was the policy evolved?
- Who administers the policy?
- Who maintains the records and copes with administration?

What do your findings suggest about the 'hidden costs of autonomy'?

Our comments

Your answers to the above questions depend to a large extent upon the scale of operation of your school or college and the frequency with which individual functions are undertaken. Although larger organizations, such as FE colleges, are able to create their own specialist personnel function this may be costly. Smaller schools and colleges may well experience problems in developing and maintaining specialist areas of personnel knowledge and expertise and finding the time to undertake the work. They may choose to buy in services formerly provided by the LEA. In turn this may create disadvantages for the school or college because of the LEA's remoteness from the situation. The development of GM primary school clusters may well lead to a shared personnel function, offering some economy of scale. Overall, however, the involvement of governors and senior staff in these functions can result in difficulties if a clear distinction between the creation of policy and day-to-day administration is not maintained.

Key learning points

- As 'service' organizations, schools and colleges depend for their success on the commitment and capability of staff. This dependence is reflected in the increased use of public domain performance indicators for teaching and support staff.
- More effective recruitment, training and development of currently 'inactive' teaching staff would help mitigate the effects of shortages expected as a result of demographic changes and competition for staff from other sectors.

- Autonomous schools and colleges enjoy greater freedom and responsibilities in all areas of HRM as a result of which they are able to develop customized approaches to the management of staff, geared to the needs and circumstances of the individual institution.

4. People or performance?

Introduction

The period since 1979, in England and Wales, has seen the development of frameworks for the inspection of school and college performance, taxonomies of professional and managerial competence and comparative data in the form of published league tables of standardized assessment test (SATs) and public examination results. The curricula which schools and colleges are required to facilitate are either prescribed via statutory national curriculum (NC) programmes of study or, in the case of vocational curricula, are determined by funding and validating bodies. Performance standards for autonomous schools and colleges, it may be argued, are increasingly centrally controlled by national government or government appointed quango. You will have noticed, no doubt, that your personal observations on your own teaching and managerial performance are increasingly measured against a framework of external expectations of performance. In addition, students and parents are encouraged to choose between competitor institutions on the basis of comparisons of actual and expected levels of performance rather than on the content of the curriculum.

At the same time, studies of management effectiveness in mainstream (e.g. Peters and Waterman, 1982) and educational organizations (e.g. Caldwell and Spinks, 1992) suggest that effective management is characterized by an ability and willingness to devolve authority and responsibility throughout the organization so that individuals and teams are 'empowered' to act.

The philosophical and empirical bases for these exhortations reflect the notion that uniquely bureaucratic styles of management with their tight control and detailed assessments of performance are unlikely to secure optimum levels of staff performance.

Advocates of people-oriented management approaches argue for supportive yet challenging styles of management. These are perceived as particularly appropriate in professionally staffed schools and colleges and a necessary response to curriculum and administrative overload in autonomous institutions.

This section examines the issues which confront managers in education in terms of responding to conflicting pressures for increased levels of public accountability and an appropriate degree of professional autonomy.

Study focus

At the end of this section you should be able to:

- summarize the tensions between the two approaches;
- analyse the management implications of each approach;
- identify which approach(es) are used in your institution;
- recognize that a combination of approaches may be needed.

Performance-centred approaches

The appearance of frameworks for the analysis of teaching or management performance reflects the trend in education towards more public or market oriented forms of accountability. Bush (1994) analyses recent changes in the balance of accountability in education. His commentary demonstrates that, in particular since the 1988 Education Reform Act, there has been a substantive *increase* in the accountability of schools and colleges to external stakeholders. Such increases have been paralleled by a *diminution* in the scope, relevance, and perceived importance of professional forms of accountability. The shift is significant. It reflects not only a more active role for central government and parents, as customers, in the definition of appropriate standards and the scrutiny of actual levels of performance, but also it emphasizes what sociologists of education, in particular, have called the attempted 'proletarianization' of teaching (e.g. Aronowitz and Giroux, 1985). In this teachers are seen primarily as 'technicians' whose job is to implement closely defined curricula which have been determined elsewhere rather than as active professionals who are regarded, like other professions, as self-determining, self-regulating, self-monitoring, and self-managing. The 'technician' analogy is most acute in the further education sector where the Further Education Funding Council (FEFC) and Training and Enterprise Councils (TECs) are seen to 'commission' the delivery of accredited vocational courses at regional and local levels with funding linked, at least in part, to successful student outcomes. Similar analogies may be drawn in relation to the development of the National Curriculum in England and Wales.

Below we briefly consider four perspectives on performance oriented approaches. These are:

- Management by objectives
- Managerial competences
- Ofsted framework
- Value-added measures.

They differ in the extent to which performance standards in each approach are:

a) internally generated
b) customized
c) developmentally oriented
d) confidential

❑ Management by objectives (MBO)

Squire (1989) argues that MBO provides an objective and necessary bulwark against both imposed performance standards and subjective or hearsay assessments of performance. For Squire MBO is essentially 'a system within which to carry out one's intentions' (p.20). The basic framework for MBO is defined by Schuster and Kindall (1974, cited in Fidler and Cooper 1988, p.4):

1. performance goals or targets initiated periodically by the employee;

2. mutual agreement on a set of goals by the employee and his [*sic*] superior after discussion;

3. periodic review by the employee and his [*sic*] superior of the match between goals and achievements.

Clearly the framework is skeletal in management terms. In relation to the work of schools and colleges there is no indication of how tensions between individual, team and whole institution objectives might be reconciled. Nor is there any reference to tangible support for training and development needs which arise from the target-setting process. Nevertheless the language of the framework is indicative of an attempt to address the issues contributing to potential antipathy we discused earlier. In that sense 'the approach is readily applicable in the education sector because, used appropriately, it values both professional "voice" and managerial responsibility' (O'Neill 1994a, p.217).

❑ Managerial competences

If MBO can be defined as an internal institutional vehicle for agreeing targets and measuring progress towards meeting those targets, then the managerial competences movement (e.g. Esp, 1993) offers a different perspective on the management of performance because it relies on a, largely external, detailed analysis of the *tasks* which might be carried out by people at various levels of responsibility within the 'typical' school or college. Task analysis is also perceived to help identify differences in levels of performance from, say, adequate to outstanding. The analysis leads to a statement of tasks or competences against which individual, or team, performance, and quality of performance might be measured. Earley (1993) implies that, whilst the competences are derived from, and relate to, actual workplace activities, the approach offers considerable possibilities when used for developmental rather than accountability purposes:

- it emphasizes workplace performance;
- it establishes an infrastructure which encourages and enables development to take place;
- it is driven by practitioners rather than trainer providers;
- it allows for better identification of training and development needs;
- it provides a higher profile for career or personal development planning;
- it empowers and motivates individuals to use the standards in ways which reflect their own needs and those of the schools in which they work;
- it enables external inputs to be identified and tailored to an individual's or a school's development plan (Earley 1993, p.110).

Whilst the approach is seen to have some advantages, critics argue that at an operational level it is time-consuming and expensive both to set up and administer, and generic rather than customized in its approach. More significantly, perhaps, competences are seen as a problematic vehicle for identifying or developing the higher order, creative, adaptive management skills which will be at a premium in autonomous schools and colleges (Burgoyne, 1989).

❏ Ofsted framework

In England and Wales the Framework for the Inspection of Schools (Ofsted, 1993a) encapsulates attempts to define generic criteria against which performance might be assessed both within and between institutions. Significantly, the purpose and focus of inspection are not on staff performance *per se* but, rather:

> The purpose of inspection is to identify strengths and weaknesses in schools so that they may improve the quality of education offered and raise the standards achieved by their pupils. Particular attention is paid to pupils' standards of achievement which are better or worse in any subject or area of learning than the average for their age and to reasons for such differences (p.4).

The emphasis of the Framework is on the contribution of teaching and management to enhanced educational outcomes whilst the criteria explicitly focus on norm-referenced standards of student attainment. In this sense staff performance is evaluated in terms of 'the quality of teaching provided and its effects on the quality of learning and standards of pupils' achievements' (p.27). The perspective is clearly one of external accountability in which priority is given to educational attainments, or outcomes, rather than to the process of teaching and learning in its own right. In Drucker's (1988) terms the quality of education is measured according to results not good intentions. However, assessments of performance which are based purely on raw data or normative criteria can be misleading. Hence we turn to the fourth option for the measurement of performance, the concept of value-added.

❏ Value-added measures

> Published league tables have been criticized for being based on raw examination results and not taking account of the nature of the intake of pupils into the school. There have been calls for more sensitive measures of schools' and colleges' performance and in particular for the use of a 'value-added' approach to examination results (Ofsted and Audit Commission 1993, p.8).

The argument for value-added approaches to the measurement of teaching and management effectiveness relates to the, quite logical, notion that student attainment, whether on entry to formal schooling at 4+ or on completion at 16, is extremely varied. In this sense the use of raw data to measure institutional or individual teacher effectiveness is too crude an approach. Hence the need to develop procedures which assess attainment on entry in order to measure 'distance travelled' by students, rather than simply linking effectiveness with student outcomes.

However, the difficulties of applying value-added approaches to the assessment of staff performance are considerable. They also create the potential for disenfranchisement of certain categories of student:

> For a number of management functions within a school or college, including staff appraisal, it is useful to know whether an abnormal level of achievement by students is partially explained by the students' prior ability. And if performance-related pay is introduced for teachers and lecturers, the use of value-added evaluations may help prevent perverse effects. If performance-related pay were determined without reference to initial attainment, teachers and lecturers with less promising intakes would receive less bonus than their counterparts in other schools or colleges. This would make teachers and lecturers less willing to work with less promising students, and institutions serving such students would become doubly disadvantaged (ibid., pp.64–65).

Activity 4.1 (A)

Consider the extent to which the four possible performance-centred approaches are used within your school or college. For what particular purposes are the various approaches used? List the advantages and disadvantages of each approach as used within your institution.

Our comments

Most schools and colleges are likely to use a combination of approaches, either by coincidence or design. The effectiveness of each approach, and the extent to which it is used, depends on:

- its acceptability to the staff concerned;
- the availability of valid and reliable data to inform assessments; and
- an understanding of the ways in which performance may be enhanced via assessment.

We consider the issues of performance management in detail in our sections on **Mentoring** and **Appraisal**.

People-oriented approaches

Elliott and Hall (1994) offer a strident critique of the way in which, in their view, 'hard' HRM approaches, which categorize people as just another resource to be manipulated in pursuit of organizational objectives, have apparently been adopted with enthusiasm by senior managers within the further education sector, post-incorporation. They point to deteriorating conditions of service for full-time staff and potential exploitation of hourly-paid staff as indicators of an inappropriate emphasis on outcomes, or performance, at the expense of people.

At the same time, we argue, the emergence of educational institutions as wild (Carlson, 1975) or open organizations which have to compete and survive in an increasingly turbulent economic, demographic and educational environment reinforces our basic premise (p.4) that schools and colleges depend for their success on the people who work there. People-oriented, as opposed to performance-oriented, perspectives may be likened to a 'soft' HRM approach. This suggests that:

> [...] employees cannot be treated just like any of the other resources because, unlike them, people think and react. There is more of an emphasis on strategies for gaining commitment by informing employees about the company's mission, values, plans and trading conditions; involving them in deciding how tasks should be carried out; and grouping them in teams which work without strict supervision (Armstrong 1991, p.35).

In addition, the general move towards HRM approaches, with a consequent emphasis on the role of the line manager, has considerable implications for the development of higher order interpersonal and communication skills in all types of organization (O'Neill, 1994b). In schools and colleges, particularly in light of perceptible trends towards flexible, independent and life-long student learning, these skills are at a premium not only in staff–staff relationships, but also in interactions between staff and students, and also between staff and the host of other stakeholders who form part of the institution's educational community. (See Colin Riches, *Communication*, Chapter 12 in the core text).

The importance of motivation

In our introduction we set out our understanding of the symbiotic relationship between individual performance and organizational effectiveness. We also suggested that optimum levels of commitment and performance were entirely contingent on management effectiveness: commitment and performance have to be actively managed rather than simply be assumed or left to chance. Underpinning this notion of affecting and improving the performance capability of individuals is the concept of motivation. Riches (1994a) implies that the concept is multi-faceted and, as such, eludes satisfactory definition. Nevertheless, he argues, the importance of motivation to autonomous schools and colleges lies both in the recognition that people are the key resource and in an awareness that training and development are key elements in promoting enhanced levels of motivation amongst, and contributions from, staff.

👁 Reading 5
Colin Riches *Motivation* Chapter 11.

Please now read the complete chapter. As you read, compare the various theories of motivation to the actual staff management strategies which are employed in your school or college. You may find it helpful to distinguish between performance- and people-oriented strategies.

Our comments

Riches summarizes the management implications of theories of motivation as follows:

- Effective organizations should expect much from the people who work for them. Low expectations are certainly demotivating in the long run and will not help the school or college overall;
- Managers must ensure that a sense of satisfaction is gained in return for effort;
- Satisfaction will derive in part from meaningful work which members are capable of and in part from managers taking pains to reward performance. Managers need to ensure that they understand what influences each individual to be satisfied, or otherwise, in her/his employment;
- Managers should encourage staff to set specific, challenging, but realistic goals for high performance by them. Consultation and training are needed to ensure commitment to these goals;
- Feedback on work performance helps staff to effective task strategies and to be motivated towards self-efficacy and to reveal discrepancies between the goal set and present performance. (p.239)

It is significant that, in linking motivation to management strategies, Riches highlights challenging goals, adequate support and training and feedback on performance as essential elements for promoting job satisfaction. Each of these, as we discuss later, is an important part of effective schemes for the induction, mentoring and appraisal of staff.

People-oriented approaches are significant in educational management because they advocate the use of a range of motivational strategies depending on the needs of the individual. For some those needs will be satisfied by purely pecuniary rewards, for others responsibility and autonomy will act as motivating factors, for yet others it will be regular and tangible recognition of performance within the team which will be paramount.

For some teachers the prospect of negotiating individual job descriptions and performance targets with performance-related pay will be an appealing prospect. For others the quality of welfare, grievance and professional association support will impact significantly on their perceptions about the quality of their working environment. O'Neill (1994a) identifies a range of factors which are available to individual institutions to respond to the needs of individuals and groups of staff within the school or college. These are shown in Figure 4.1.

Remuneration	Welfare	Development
starting salary	incapacity benefits	induction
salary progression	career-break entitlements	mentoring
performance-related pay	child-care provision	appraisal
	security of tenure	opportunities for career and professional development
	retirement provision	
	grievance and discipline mechanisms	
	counselling	
	working conditions	
	union recognition	
	redundancy	

Figure 4.1 Factors in the management of staff commitment (O'Neill 1994a, p.215)

Equally, people-oriented approaches acknowledge the extrinsic nature of motivation in that it depends on feedback and support from others within the team or wider institution. Hence Morgan (1989) sees the change of management emphasis not so much in terms of a people-versus-performance debate but, rather, as an issue of appropriate management style:

> We have been through a phase of 'macho management' in which a highly analytical, directive, 'top-down' approach has dominated. Now we seem to be moving into a phase where more empathic, relationship-oriented approaches, based on co-operation rather than competition, are often more appropriate. Here, women often have the better record (p.37).

Coleman (1994, p.194) argues that such changes in management style are a topical issue in education given that:

> [...] there is a growing recognition that those gender qualities identified with the feminine side of human nature are amongst those required in the management of the effective school.

Organizational culture

We would argue that such a view, whilst helpful, fails to take account of the special professional context which exists in educational organizations and which directly influences levels of individual and organizational performance. In this sense an understanding of organizational culture contributes substantially to our awareness of how people in organizations arrive at an understanding of what standards of performance are expected, rather than demanded, of them.

At its most simplistic level, the effect of organizational culture on individuals may be represented in terms of values, norms and behaviours (Figure 4.2).

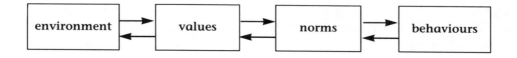

Figure 4.2 The development of organizational culture (O'Neill 1994c, p.104)

O'Neill (1994c, p.105) contends that:

> Values and norms inform the behaviour of organizational members. Equally changes in behaviour help modify established norms and values. Hence, tangible manifestations of culture are of primary importance within the organization. They help to promote and reinforce that translation of cultural values into appropriate norms and behaviours.

From this perspective it is possible to argue that the behaviour, or performance, of individuals will be influenced not only by the range of motivational strategies outlined by Riches above, but also by the *de facto* behavioural norms which apply within the school or college. Staff, by virtue of the fact that they work within the institution, experience, at first hand, the standards of performance and quality of relationships which are the norm. They can can also be aware of the levels of performance and interpersonal relationships which are actually expected of them as individuals. In our section on **Induction** we emphasize the importance of the socialization and cultural integration of new members of staff.

We can make an important distinction between what the organization promotes in terms of institutional values and norms, and what individuals perceive to be values and norms 'on the ground'. In short, it is possible that in any given educational establishment there will be a discrepancy between policy and practice. In such a scenario it is likely that individual behaviour will conform with actual practice rather than official policy. Thus whilst people-oriented approaches are helpful inasmuch as they highlight the variety of individual needs which contribute to enhanced motivation and commitment, they need to be understood within an organizational context which suggests that levels of individual performance are also affected to a significant degree by the prevailing culture of the institution.

Activity 4.2 (A) (C)

Research tool: critical incidents diary

Maintain a critical incidents diary for a week of activities when you are involved with other staff. An entry might look something like this:

> **Mon. Late morning.** Discussion with classroom assistant about the possibility of her participating in area training course to increase her display skills. She was reluctant to miss hearing individual children read as planned.

At the end of the week classify the incidents according to the list of five 'management implications' enumerated above by Riches (p.25). This particular entry would be an example of the fourth implication:

> Managers should encourage staff to set specific, challenging, but realistic goals for high performance by them. Consultation and training are needed to ensure commitment to these goals.

What do your findings tell you about the organizational culture of the school or college?

The critical incidents diary is a research tool which enables us to chart events as they happen and then reflect upon them, classify them and relate them to a theoretical background. You will find, no doubt, that this tool is problematic — time for completion doesn't always occur when it is needed!

Our comments

Your diary may show that the school or college is one which presents many opportunities for people to feel that they and their work are valued and developed within an encouraging positive environment. Equally, you may feel that an appropriate range of motivational strategies is lacking in your situation, or indeed, that motivational strategies are employed with some groups of staff and not with others.

Management implications

We conclude this section with an assessment of the issues which need to be addressed by schools and colleges in their attempts to resolve the people-versus-performance debate. Significantly, in referring to the work of Bosetti (1994) in Canada, we end by returning to the 'management of learning' implications of the debate.

1.   Drucker (1988, p.362) argues that the guiding principle for any policy or action in the management of staff has to be that of integrity; decisions which relate to the management of staff have to be consistent with the values espoused by the institution, and not, by implication, governed by considerations of expediency. This is a significant polemic in educational management because schools and colleges are subject to powerful external financial and accountability constraints which, at times, conflict with historical staffing structures and accepted norms concerning conditions of service. The concerns articulated above (p.24) by Elliott and Hall reflect the potential hazards of a management approach which emphasizes efficiency and outcomes at the expense of individual welfare. Equally, however, Drucker explicitly links integrity with a concern for high performance standards. Inappropriate standards of performance, he suggests, should not be ignored but must be actively confronted and addressed, so that organizations develop a norm of high expectations of performance and achievement. This issue is a major consideration in our section on **Appraisal**.

2.   We have already highlighted the view that performance standards are not absolute (p.5). They are, rather, dependent on context and a host of organizational and environmental variables which militate against the simplistic comparison of performance both within and between institutions. At the heart of the process of defining performance standards are the issues of ownership and fitness-for-purpose.

Bosetti's study in Alberta, Canada, for example, criticizes the District Authority's externally imposed policy for the evaluation of teacher performance:

> It therefore remained disconnected from other school and district policies and professional development activities. Conducted by school principals, and used to monitor teacher performance and for administrative decisions regarding personnel and contractual matters, it reinforced hierarchical relationships, and tended to be anti-professional in nature. Instead of using the process to hold teachers accountable for their professional judgement in creating quality learning activities that met the intellectual needs of students, in practice it was more aimed at holding teachers accountable for following standard operational procedures (Bosetti 1994, p.59).

Key learning points

- External forms of accountability and published performance standards are routine aspects of the management of autonomous schools and colleges; studies of management effectiveness suggest that empowerment and autonomy for staff are important contributors to internal organizational effectiveness.
- An insistence on high standards of performance and a concern for the differing needs of individual staff are complementary, rather than conflicting, aspects of the effective management of human resources.
- Optimum levels of individual performance are contingent upon effective management which is characterized by support, feedback on performance and higher order interpersonal skills.
- Individual motivation to perform is informed and constrained by an understanding of organizational values and norms.

5. Individual and organizational development

Introduction

The existence of a causal relationship between optimum individual performance and an effective framework of organizational support is central to the principles of human resource management. Whilst the management of classroom teaching and learning at the point where teacher and child interact may, in your experience, be largely a solitary professional role, the broader range of administrative and managerial tasks which you undertake within the institution are collaborative activities; you will normally work as a member of one or more groups or teams in the pursuit of common objectives.

Professional development in these terms can be seen as purposive, as part of that framework of organizational support, the objective of which is to help integrate the development of individuals within the work of the organization. The integration of people's work and development in educational organizations is thus the major focus for this section.

Study focus

At the end of this section you should be able to:

- identify the principal issues in managing professional development;
- recognize the links between individual and organizational development;
- be aware of the importance of the effective and efficient integration of staff.

The importance of integration

We can suggest several reasons which help to explain the emergence of integration as a key management issue in both individual and organizational development:

1. In autonomous schools and colleges, traditional staffing structures and historical divisions between professional and other types of work are increasingly being called into question (e.g. Mortimore et al., 1992).

2. External accountability and resource efficiency factors have led to organizations in all sectors being less tolerant of what Riches (1994a) labels organizational 'slack', thus schools and colleges are exhorted to ensure appropriate levels of contribution from all individuals and groups within the organization.

3. The increasing complexity of the management of learning in the 1990s, reflected in the use of a more diverse range of teaching and learning styles, rapid developments in the content and skills specifications for areas of learning and greater sophistication in the assessment and recording of individual student learning, creates significant organizational difficulties in terms of managers attempting to simultaneously support individual, curriculum and whole-institution development.

4. The massive increase in information processing demanded of autonomous schools and colleges, combined with the very real need for higher order interpersonal and communication skills in working

relationships, serve to underline the importance of effective communication networks and procedures in educational organizations. In this sense the concept of integration embraces both the relationships between people within the school or college and the work they do.

In the sections on **Induction** and **Mentoring** we consider these issues in greater detail.

◉ Reading 6

John O'Neill *Managing Professional Development* Chapter 14.

Please read the first part of the chapter up to, but not including, 'Learning theory and style'. As you read, note:
- *the relationship between development for individuals and organizations;*
- *potential tensions associated with control of professional development; and*
- *the differences in development need associated with stages in career.*

Our comments

The reading highlights the importance of:

- appropriate needs analysis;
- the need to integrate individual and organizational learning; and
- the complexities of providing meaningful development opportunities for all staff within the institution.

We begin this part of the section by looking briefly at the range of tensions associated with organizational development identified by Dalin (1993), and then proceed to examine how the work of the school or college might be organized to facilitate such integration and development. The relationship between teamwork and development is analyzed in depth. The latter parts of the section consider issues associated with the management of accountability and development.

Organizational development

Dalin's extensive work on institutional development in northern Europe, principally in Norway, the Netherlands and Germany, has identified effective human relations between all members of the school community as a key determinant of school quality. Certain institutional 'dilemmas' are enumerated:

- How can 'membership' really be felt, even when personal values, personality and norms are different from those of the majority?
- How are feelings expressed? Can a school accept all forms of feelings (and their expression)? And how can one be fair? (For example, do we treat boys and girls alike?)
- Do we accept that all members, students as well as leaders, have the right to influence, and how can we deal with unacceptable ways of using influence (by leaders, teachers and students)?
- Does the school have an open and constructive communication process at all levels, or is energy blocked because people do not talk to each other?
- How does the school deal with conflicts and problem-solving? Does it have acceptable procedures and norms or are these *ad hoc* or non-existent?
- Is the school working with its own culture and climate, and are 'process' issues accepted, as well as discussions of content? (Dalin 1993, p.9)

These management dilemmas, albeit expressed in broad terms, provide a useful agenda for individual and organizational development from an HRM perspective. In particular they reinforce the importance of the following issues:

- appropriate and effective **communication** processes;
- full **integration** of all organizational members;
- positive **resolution of conflict**;
- a **code of conduct** which reflects the organization's **culture**; and
- appropriate degrees of **involvement in decision-making**.

Such issues are complex in terms of overall school and college management. Decisions, for example, about the form and content of induction, mentoring and appraisal schemes may challenge existing values and norms within the institution. Nevertheless, the issues can, for the purposes of our discussions here, be reduced to an analysis of how work might be organized in institutions to promote the integration of individuals within the work of the organization and continuous organizational improvement.

Managing integration

An appropriate starting point, then, would seem to be Everard and Morris's (1990) matrix, below, which sets individual learning and improvement within the context of team and organizational performance.

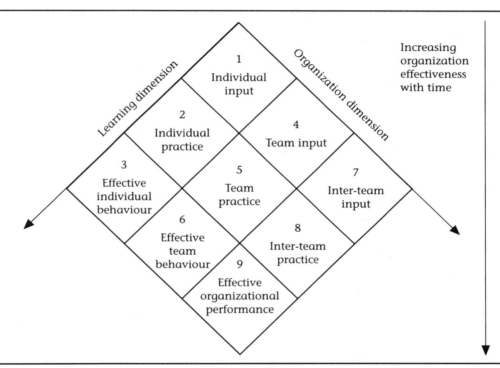

Figure 5.1 Training and organization development matrix (Reprinted with permission of the authors, Everard and Morris 1990, p.173)

The central importance of teams and teamwork is a basic premise of the matrix which is itself a helpful contribution to our conceptual understanding of the way effective organizations develop. The key elements here are that:

a) organizations depend for their development on the effective practice of individuals and teams which make up the organization;
b) individual learning takes place within the structured work of the team;
c) organizational development depends on the effective integration of the various teams which operate within the organization.

◎ Reading 7

Coleman, M. and Bush, T. *Managing with Teams* Chapter 13.

Please now read the latter sections of this chapter, from 'Developing effective teams'. As you read, note the complexities associated with promoting meaningful teamwork in schools and colleges.

Our comments

As you will be aware from your own experience in education, effective teamwork may not be a readily attainable norm in many institutions. You may find it difficult to see how teamwork might be developed in your institution without the existence of certain preconditions.

We turn now to an exploration of how some of these tensions associated with teamwork might be addressed within the institution.

Teamwork

Coleman and Bush highlight the notion of interdependence between **managing with** teams and **development for** those teams:

> If teams are to play an important role in the management of schools and colleges and operate effectively, the ways in which members are selected, and the opportunities for team building and development, are particularly significant (Coleman and Bush 1994, p.283).

Below, we offer three examples of how groups of professional staff in schools and colleges have been encouraged to engage in collaborative work and learning and, as a result, develop characteristics associated with effective teamwork.

Stevenson and Stigler (1992), in their study of Japanese practice, emphasize the role of the institution in developing professional, i.e. teaching and learning, competence amongst colleagues:

> Japanese teachers, beginners as well as seasoned teachers, are required to perfect their teaching skills through interaction with other teachers. For instance, meetings are organized by the vice-principal and headteachers at their school. These experienced professionals assume responsibility for advising and guiding their young colleagues. The headteachers also organize meetings to discuss teaching techniques and to devise lesson plans and handouts. These discussions are very pragmatic and are aimed both at developing better teaching techniques and at constructing plans for specific lessons (Stevenson and Stigler, cited in Fullan 1993, p.133).

This approach has some similarities with that advocated by the Further Education Unit's (FEU) review of the use of quality circles for staff development (FEU, 1989). They suggest the purpose of quality circles is:

> that small volunteer groups of workers meet for an hour a week with a trained leader, operating to a strict code of conduct, to consider work related problems and recommend solutions which are then implemented, unless there are good reasons for not doing so (FEU 1989, p.1).

Their comparison of quality circles in two colleges is helpful in highlighting the management issues associated with linking staff development and institutional problem-solving in this way:

> The differing experiences at Accrington and Rossendale College and Barnfield College illustrate how quality circles might be used as an approach to staff development as well as a way of solving problems. There are

common themes — the need for a facilitator for each circle; the need for the support of management, especially middle management; and a need for participants to feel that their recommendations would be considered by management and appropriate action taken (ibid., p.4).

It is possible to extrapolate three key points of tension based on the effects of testing the theory of quality circles in college practice:

- the key role played by middle managers;
- the need for effective communication at all levels within the institution;
- the need for clarity concerning authority to act.

Based on their experience of 'learning networks' in Enfield Local Education Authority, Goddard and Clinton (1994) argue that an environment for development can be further encouraged by interaction and collaboration between institutions:

> A learning environment provides the framework for the teacher and the school to change and improve. A learning network between institutions opens up the creative and learning opportunities and ultimately benefits the institution. For small schools, linkages across schools is essential if any viable learning environment is to be created. The viability of networks depends on being able to bring together enough people to create the motivation, capacity and creative energy to be productive (Goddard and Clinton 1994, p.59).

In these three examples integration occurs as individuals take on meaningful work within various groups within the institution. Individual and organizational development are seen to be symbiotic:

- the common **process** is effective group or teamwork;
- the **critical success factor** in terms of organizational development is the linking together of the work of different operating units.

By implication we can argue that it is at the level of inter-team practice, to use the terminology of the Everard and Morris matrix, that communication networks and procedures are most significant, whilst within individual teams consensus around goals, purposeful leadership and higher-order interpersonal skills are called for.

Activity 5.1 (R) (A)

Outline the ways in which integration and development of staff take place within your school or college. Consider both the informal networks and formal processes which facilitate or inhibit integration. Summarize in one sentence a proposed change which might lead to more effective integration.

Our comments

Your response may well indicate that official integration occurs through induction and mentoring schemes, existing departmental team structures, membership of working groups, and cross-school or college groups involved with the management of, for example, pastoral care, assessment and record-keeping or student support. Unofficial integration may well arise from friendship networks and voluntary activities such as a school trip or fundraising event. It is important to realize that the way individuals and groups develop within the institution will be influenced by both official and unofficial processes. Equally it is important to note that integration and development can, and do, take place outside formal training programmes.

We have identified two further variables which are closely associated with development via integration and teamwork. Thus, we turn now to an exploration of how organizational size and complexity and organizational maturity affect development.

Organizational size and complexity

The Everard and Morris matrix remains an attractive model for the simultaneous promotion of individual and organizational development yet, at the level of inter-team practice, it is highly problematic. Empirical studies in schools in England and Wales have demonstrated the difficulties, in particular, of ensuring the integration of different teams within the one organization.

> One of the criteria by which senior staff identified effective middle managers, and a quality which was highly valued, was the ability to take a wide perspective and see subject or area concerns in the context of the whole school. Middle managers who fought for their own corner regardless of the needs of colleagues in other departments and whole school policies were regarded unfavourably (Earley and Fletcher Campbell 1992, p.192).

This notion is reinforced by Bolam et al. (1993) whose study of management practice in primary and secondary schools emphasized the importance of organizational **size** and **complexity** as contributory factors to the level of integration and general organizational effectiveness.

> Primary schools have relatively small and simple structures which are probably relatively easy to co-ordinate, whereas secondary schools are relatively large, complex and less easy to co-ordinate at school level, but probably more tightly structured and easier to co-ordinate at department level. It may well be the case, therefore, that primary headteachers and teachers are more likely to have a shared understanding of the various aspects of school management than their secondary colleagues, whereas the latter are more likely to have that understanding at departmental level. There was some evidence that subject departments were the key management structures in secondary schools but there was little evidence of inter-departmental collaboration (Bolam et al. 1993, pp.124–125).

This relationship has been recognized and addressed outside education for many years. (See John O'Neill, *Organizational Structure and Culture*, Chapter 5.) In autonomous schools and colleges the integration imperative we outlined above has led to a questioning of traditional views concerning the optimum size and structure for educational organizations (Handy and Aitken, 1986; Beare et al., 1989).

To size and complexity we might add the concept of organizational **maturity** as a third significant influence in relation to the effective integration and development of staff at organizational level.

Organizational maturity

Dalin's management dilemmas we referred to earlier in this section (p.30) are potentially very threatening for schools and colleges inasmuch as they call into question the extent of control, by which we mean autonomy and authority, which teachers and managers are willing to devolve in their management of student learning, *within the institution*. Further, the relative willingness of staff in an institution to engage in meaningful review and analysis of the way learning is organized, delivered and supported is a key indicator of organizational maturity. The notion of maturity is explained in Hoyle and McCormick's (1976) distinction between restricted and extended professionality, illustrated in Figure 5.2.

According to their typology, a norm of extended professionality is more likely to promote development for individuals, and to rely on the very inter-team practice which is deemed essential for integration and development at whole school or college level. It is legitimate to argue, for example, that the existence of

Restricted professionality	Extended professionality
Skills derived from experience	Skills derived from a mediation between experience and theory
Perspective limited to the immediate in time and place	Perspective embracing the broader social context of education
Classroom events perceived in isolation	Classroom events perceived in relation to school policies and goals
Introspective with regard to methods	Methods compared with those of colleagues and with reports of practice
Value placed on autonomy	Value placed on professional collaboration
Limited involvement in non-teaching professional activities	High involvement in non-teaching professional activities (esp. teachers' centres, subject associations, research)
Infrequent reading of professional literature	Regular reading of professional literature
Involvement in in-service work limited and confined to practical courses	Involvement in in-service work considerable and includes courses of a theoretical nature
Teaching as an intuitive activity	Teaching seen as a rational activity

Figure 5.2 Restricted and extended models of professionality (Hoyle and McCormick 1976, p.75)

meaningful and challenging schemes for the induction and mentoring of staff are tangible indicators of a mature school or college. These concepts of maturity or extended professionality are also directly linked to the belief that mistakes are an essential element of learning and optimum levels of individual performance which we discussed earlier (p.6).

From an organizational perspective the work of Nias et al. (1989) in England and that of Hopkins (1987) internationally add a useful dimension to our understanding of extended professionality for they illustrate:

- the importance of organizational culture as a **context** for interpreting professionality; and
- the need for an appropriate **process** to enable staff to enhance their ability to promote more effective management of learning.

Activity 5.2 (A)

List those features of size and complexity which help and hinder integration of the various working units within your school or college. What would now be your priority for action?

Our comments

You will perhaps have concluded that numbers of staff, their relative physical isolation from each other, timetable arrangements and competing work demands are negative aspects of size which hinder both development work and more general integration. The great advantage of size is that it can provide some economies of scale in terms of management and administration.

The features of complexity you have identified may be related to competition for resources, interpersonal or group relationships and management or organizational structures. Your priority for action might be the most significant issue or, conversely, the most readily changed feature. But which would be the most effective?

A context for organizational improvement

Nias et al. (1989) identified, in their study based on a sample of 'successful' primary schools, a 'culture of collaboration' which was perceived to provide an appropriate environment or context for individual and whole-school work and development. Key elements of this culture were openness, professional and personal interdependence, a valuing of groupwork, and strong leadership. In terms of organizational development, these norms were seen to lead to self-confidence and resilience within the school:

> Heads and staff were reasonably assured that what they were doing was, in their own terms, right. This was partly because the leaders were convinced that their mission was appropriate to the school and the children in it and partly because it was shared by the majority of the staff group. Both factors were instrumental in creating strong, self-confident corporate cultures (Nias et al. 1989, p.185).

These observations are in sympathy with Fullan's (1991) assertion about people's capacity to change: 'It isn't that people resist change as much as they don't know how to cope with it' (Fullan 1991, p.xiv).

Strongly articulated school and college cultures would appear both to facilitate integration and to provide the appropriate **context** for change and development (Beare et al., 1989; O'Neill, 1994c). In the age of autonomous schools, however, an effective **process** for organizational improvement is as topical and important an issue as context.

The processes adopted for organizational development in autonomous schools and colleges must meet the twin demands of external accountability and internal credibility. Thus we turn now to an examination of how educational organizations might purposefully work towards institutional improvement and satisfy both sets of demands.

The two examples we analyse below are both concerned with institutional review and development; both rely for their success on the active commitment of the staff involved. They differ, however, in their orientation; in the first there is a major accountability emphasis, in the second there is a much greater staff development focus.

Organizational improvement and external accountability

In South Australia institutional development and external accountability have become closely associated concepts, through a comparable approach to that prescribed in England and Wales via the Ofsted Framework for the Inspection of Schools. The process of school review adopted in South Australia also focuses on learning outcomes but with a distinctive emphasis.

> The overall goals of school reviews are concerned with development and accountability. Development is examined through a focus on the extent to which the school has achieved the outcomes stated in the school development plans. Accountability is pursued through the external review procedures that provide information about management structures and processes which impact on effectiveness, allowing weaknesses, and strategies for improvement, to be identified (Ofsted 1993b, p.2).

One significant difference, however, between the Australian system and that adopted in England and Wales is the membership of the review team. In South Australia serving teachers are seconded to the Education Review Unit (ERU) which carries out school reviews. In addition, the principal of the institution under review also becomes a member of the review team. The benefits of such an approach are perceived to be considerable, including an enhanced sense of ownership of the review process by the institutions themselves.

> The credibility of teams and the acceptability of their findings by professionals are greatly enhanced by the secondment of serving teachers to the ERU for one or two terms and their subsequent return to the classroom. Thus a significant number of schools reviewed have by now had a member of staff at some time seconded to the ERU and those carrying out the reviews will themselves have been reviewed in the past. This system strengthens

the feeling of collaborative working towards improvement. It also helps the reviewers and reviewed together to identify key issues and seek for acceptable solutions (ibid., p.7).

A workable balance between development and accountability perspectives is perceived as highly desirable in the South Australia system of school review. We have already discussed, in our **People or Performance** section, the issue of accountability and performance-centred approaches to the management of staff. We turn now to the relationship between institutional review as *process* and professional development.

Organizational improvement and professional development

The Everard and Morris matrix rightly emphasizes the need to develop individuals within teams and to integrate, where appropriate, the work of different teams in pursuit of organizational development. The difficulty with the model, however, is that it offers no indication of an appropriate process to encourage that collaboration and integration. Nor, indeed, is there any suggestion of how individuals and groups of staff are to develop the requisite skills to enable them to work collaboratively. (See, for example, Colin Riches, *Communication*, Chapter 12). Here we examine one such approach:

> School Based Review (SBR) is a school improvement strategy that involves a whole school staff in a systematic review of current practice for the purpose of developing and implementing action plans for improvement. As such, SBR places great emphasis on effective staff collaboration which means that in most schools, skills in communication, problem solving, and team building have to be consciously developed (Hopkins 1987, p.154).

SBR is a process through which staff engage in an analysis of their work. It is predicated on the twin notions that:

- the staff of the institution are best placed to help the school or college review its practice and develop in a meaningful way; and
- staff need some agreed process by which they can undertake such a complex task.

The range of necessary skills, and the degree of collaboration required for the SBR process reinforce the importance of organizational maturity as a contributory factor to school or college effectiveness. Hopkins argues that the usefulness of SBR is that, in undertaking the process of review, staff use and perfect the skills which help them, individually and collectively, develop an extended professionality (Hoyle and McCormick, op. cit.) perspective on their management of learning.

Hopkins identifies several benefits of SBR:

- SBR itself is a means of staff development;
- By doing SBR, the staff will also be developing a set of specific skills;
- Optimally SBR results in the improvement of some aspect of the teaching/learning or organizational process in the school;
- SBR tends to develop an innovative orientation amongst a staff and within a school;
- The establishing of a positive climate for staff development (Hopkins 1987, pp.165–167).

Hopkins also suggests that SBR will succeed only if promoted and supported by the wider educational system. We would argue that such support appears to be an integral feature of the school review system adopted in South Australia.

Organizational improvement and individual development

Implicit throughout our discussions in this section, has been the argument that individual and organizational development are closely intertwined. This is evident in the normative matrix provided by Everard and Morris (p.31) which is conceptually useful but fails to acknowledge the difficulties of integrating the work of individuals within teams or of marrying the priorities of various teams within the institution. The polemic returns us to the arguments we originally discussed in relation to the HRM versus personnel management debate. In the context of educational organizations, is individual development the responsibility of the individual, the professional tutor, the team leader or the institution as a whole?

Blanchard and Peale (1988) argue that the management of individual performance is routinely characterized by evaluation and target-setting mechanisms, but lacks any systematic approach to support for the work of the individual.

All the emphasis is on evaluation with some on performance planning but very little, if any, attention is directed towards coaching or supporting and helping employees win (Blanchard and Peale 1988, p. 100).

The polemic has ready application in the education sector. The most enduring taxonomy of the role of the primary school subject co-ordinator (Campbell, 1985) identifies time and the difficulties of observing classroom performance of colleagues as considerable constraints on the ability of teachers with 'management of learning' responsibilities to influence the work of colleagues by 'coaching'. Campbell's study in ten primary schools underlines the difficulty in all schools and colleges of engaging in professional development for individuals which attempts to link development and performance.

The School Management Task Force report (DES, 1990) provides a concise chronology of the changes in management development approaches in education. In particular they focus on:

- a move away from knowledge-based, off-site courses;
- a more explicit linkage between training or development and actual work undertaken;
- the managerial support that institutions need to provide as a matter of course for individuals in the workplace.

The change of emphasis is illustrated in Figure 5.3.

Current emphasis		Redirected emphasis
tutor-directed courses	→	support for self-directed study by individuals, school teams, peer groups
off-site training	→	in-school and near-to-the-school training
predetermined times	→	flexitime study
oral presentations	→	distance learning materials, information packs and projects
provider-determined syllabus	→	school-determined agenda
knowledge acquisition	→	performance enhancement

Figure 5.3 Changing priorities in management training provision (DES 1990, p.21)

Their perspective reinforces the idea that individual and organizational development should be synonymous with one another.

It becomes possible to regard the achievement of corporate goals and meeting the individual's needs more as matters of mutual benefit than of competing demands. For example, succession planning to forecast job vacancies and to meet future organizational requirements can improve individual career opportunities. Recognition of the need to match corporate and individual needs results in a more sharply focused approach to the selection of learning opportunities of benefit to both. School management development seen from this perspective is directly related to the effectiveness of the school and its management, as well as to the experiences of teachers and pupils. It is no longer a marginal activity. Training and development activities must be planned and implemented in the broader context of the organization (DES 1990, pp. 8–9).

Empirical studies (e.g. Campbell, 1985; Earley and Fletcher-Campbell, 1992), which scrutinize the inherent professional and interpersonal tensions associated with the management and development of individual performance by such an approach, suggest that the Task Force perspective outlined above may be remote from actual practice in many institutions. As one way forward, however, it is possible to draw on our discussions throughout this section and suggest that effective individual development requires the following preconditions to exist in schools and colleges:

- a strong and supportive organizational culture;
- a norm of extended professionality;
- a clearly defined and accepted role for line managers or team leaders; and
- a review and development process which integrates the development of individuals within the routine work of the school or college.

Activity 5.3 (R) (A) and 👁 **Reading 8**

John O'Neill *Managing Professional Development* Chapter 14.

Please read the second half of the chapter, beginning with the section 'Changing performance'.

Now apply, in detail, the SMTF approach to the way professional development provision is organized in your school or college. Begin by considering which side of the model more accurately describes exisiting provision. For example, is the emphasis on 'support for self-directed study'? Is the majority of training and development conducted 'on-site'? Are you working towards a clear, 'school-determined agenda'?

Identify, from your reading, the areas of 'support' and 'approach' which need to be modified or developed in your institution.

Our comments

You will realize that the more complex the organization the more difficult is the management of change — especially where attitudes are concerned. It may be useful for you to take the key learning points below and use them as a framework for planning staff development. However, in order to balance development and accountability priorities you will need to relate staff development to performance management. We suggest how this might be applied in practice in our section on **Appraisal** which identifies a range of strategies for managing performance.

Key learning points

- Individual and organizational development are symbiotic; teams are perceived to provide an effective vehicle for the development of both.
- Effective development is constrained by potential tensions in inter-team practice, definitions of the role of the line manager or team leader, and the closeness of the link between training and actual performance.
- The ability of individuals and organizations to develop is determined by existing norms concerning professionality and institutional culture.
- Effective development is dependent on an appropriate process to support review together with higher order communication and interpersonal skills to promote meaningful analysis of practice.

contd.

You then have the cost of the **post** in terms of what the school or college is investing in over that period:

- Now calculate the cost options involved in advertising (where? in what form?), documentation production and postage,
- travel and subsistence expenses for interviewees and interviewers,
- the opportunity cost of the time spent by interviewers and others involved in the recruitment process.

This gives you the cost of **making the appointment**.

The key cost issue for managers is in weighing the two totals against each other to reach a decision about how much to spend on recruitment.

It will be helpful to repeat the above for appointing a member of the support staff.

Our comments

Some of the early OFSTED inspection reports on secondary schools in England and Wales draw attention to the opportunity cost of making staff appointments and you may well find that your costing exercise shows that an alternative deployment of staff might be more cost effective. The core unit on *Finance and External Relations* develops this further.

Recruitment policies and procedures

A useful starting point is for us to consider an example of an actual recruitment policy taken, in this instance, from a local authority in England.

Recruitment Policy

OUR POLICIES ARE:

1. To recruit the most suitable applicant for the job.

2. To recruit ensuring that no one receives less favourable treatment on the grounds of race, colour, nationality, ethnic or national origins, disability, gender or marital status or is disadvantaged by conditions or requirements which cannot be shown to be justifiable.

3. To treat applicants as valued people keeping them informed of the processes involved and the current state of their application.

4. To use the best methods of assessment available in order to compare applicants' abilities against the job's requirements.

5. To collect and hold only sufficient data to enable the processes to be undertaken and not to use the data for any other unrelated purpose.

6. To undertake all such activities in a professional manner observing the highest possible standards of security, confidentiality and objectivity, whilst operating within the limits of available resources.

(Northamptonshire County Council, 1993)

Such a policy statement has implications for the information provided for potential applicants, arrangements for de-briefing of unsuccessful candidates, the personnel specification for the vacancy concerned, and also the treatment of internal candidates for the post. We address those implications in the discussions which now follow.

Procedures involved in managing recruitment

❑ Defining the vacancy

There are two basic areas to be managed in defining the vacancy:

- describing the job ('job description'); and
- describing the person who would best fill the job ('person[nel] specification').

Several writers on personnel issues suggest an 'exit interview' (i.e. interviewing the person who is leaving to create the vacancy) in order to ascertain why the person is leaving and establish whether the existing job and person specifications are still relevant.

> You must focus on the job to be done, not on the person who used to do it, on the needs of the children and the community, and the balance within the teaching staff as a whole — in the light of your educational aims and the school's development plans. The discussions that take place at this point will set the scene for the whole selection process. Working together as a team with the head, you (the governors) must reach decisions on what exactly you are looking for (Taylor and Hemmingway 1990, p.8).

Thomson (1993, p.12) suggests the following as ways of ascertaining what the job **actually** involves, to enable the job description to be written:

- Question the present job-holder about the job using a written questionnaire.
- Give the present job-holder a list of possible tasks and ask him/her to select those that apply to this job.
- Interview the job-holder.
- Watch the job-holder performing the job.
- Ask other people what they think the job entails.
- Ask the job-holder to keep a diary of everything he/she does in performing the job.
- Do the job yourself for a few days and keep a detailed record.
- Involve the job-holder and his/her supervisor in determining which tasks contribute positively to satisfactory completion of the job and those which inhibit satisfactory job completion (critical incident technique).

Activity 7.4 (C) and 👁 Reading 10

Attempt to gather a range of job descriptions for members of your school or college. If these are not available, interview three different people to see what they think their job descriptions should contain.

Now read again the section 'Professional development and the curriculum' in

John O'Neill *Managing Professional Development* Chapter 14,

and examine the job descriptions to see how far they recognize capability, performance, development and accountability in the post holder.

Our comments

In many examples we find that the job description is merely a set of tasks. It often ignores the practicalities of development and support for individual performance within the organization. However, in some instances the job description may include indicators of those elements of a personnel specification which may be necessary for the post in question.

❏ Person specification

A number of check lists have been devised for use in devising a person specification.

Rodger's (1952) '7-Point Plan' is one of the best known and suggests:

Physique: Health, strength, appearance, voice and other physical attributes.

Attainments: General education, job training and job experience.

General intelligence: Capacity for complex mental work, general reasoning ability.

Special aptitudes: Predisposition to acquire certain types of skill.

Interests: Inclination towards intellectual, social, practical, constructive or physically active leisure pursuits.

Disposition: Steadiness and reliability, degree of acceptability to and influence over others, self-reliance.

Circumstances: Mobility, age, domicile.

However, Hackett (1992, p.35) draws attention to the importance of the behaviour expected of the person when they are actually appointed, rather than personality traits or intellectual capability:

> A more direct approach to establishing just what you need to look for is to consider what the job-holder must be able to *do* — that is, what *abilities* he [sic] needs. If you can match these against the *demands* which the job will make, you are less likely to find that you have recruited someone who is incapable of performing to the required standard. If you also give some thought to the *rewards* which the job offers, in terms of pay and benefits, relationships and job satisfaction, you can then work out what individual *needs* these are likely to satisfy. If you recruit someone whose needs are met by the rewards which the job offers, he [sic] is much more likely to stay and work hard.

This sort of specification provides the **criteria** on which the selection will actually be based.

Activity 7.5 (R) (A)

An interesting and challenging exercise would be to devise a specification for the person required to fill your current post if you were to leave it! Does it have to be someone like you?

Our comments

No doubt we are all aware that we are indispensable! Nevertheless, it is possible that you will have realized that, when it comes to your leaving a post, it has actually changed and that, by completing this sort of exercise, you may well be contributing to an evaluation process which will help the organization.

Other issues in recruitment involve:

- the nature of the **contract** (permanent or fixed-term? full-time or part-time? job share?)
- **advertising**
- **information** to be sent to applicants

Apart from the importance of this information for recruitment purposes, it is important to realize that:

> a request for an application form represents a major opportunity to market the school [...] this opportunity must be firmly grasped (Hume 1990, p.40).

(Marketing as a management issue is dealt with more fully in Marianne Coleman, *Managing External Relations*, Chapter 18 and the associated core unit *Managing Finance and External Relations*).

In addition, part of the purpose of sending good information is for unsuitable applicants to de-select themselves, for:

> the more information you send to candidates, provided it's relevant and well-presented, then the better able they will be to decide for themselves whether it's the kind of job they're suited for. This can save you — and them — a lot of wasted time (Taylor and Hemmingway 1990, p.15).

It is worth emphasizing again that in the management of human resources, the recruitment of effective staff is inevitably concerned with certain formal procedures, some of them demanded by legislation and some by organizational 'rules'. Although this is so, the concern for **quality**, **commitment** and **performance** remains central to effective management of these procedures. Procedures offer frameworks within which effective managers perform. Equally, all kinds of key management principles are related which affect the school or college's culture, structure, environment, strategic planning and finance. We now examine three issues that may arise with particular regard to recruitment but which also relate strongly to broader issues of quality, commitment and performance.

1. Working mothers

Given the labour market context described earlier, your school or college may feel it appropriate to provide facilities for this important potential part of the labour market. There is a large Pool of Inactive Teachers (PIT) in a number of countries and the majority of them are women (Hume, 1990; Steele, 1992).

Some schools and colleges do provide creches or nursery facilities: these tend to be the larger organizations. Many smaller schools cannot afford them. In considering their options schools and colleges need to speculate on the implications of their policy, i.e. whether or not they choose to provide such facilities, for the eventual gender and age profile of the institution and, indeed, their impact on organizational culture. (See Marianne Coleman, *Women in Educational Management*, Chapter 9, for a wider examination of these issues.)

Studies of secondary and further education organizations with pre-school provision have indicated an influence on student behaviour. Clearly, the presence of these facilities also influences staff behaviour inasmuch as it has implications for 'after school' meetings, extra-curricular activities, and levels of staff motivation.

2. Internal promotion

We have referred to this in terms of succession planning but Hunt (1986) uses the term 'organizational incest' to describe an inward-looking culture.

> It is true that recruiting outsiders may upset career paths and damage egos of some employees, but the alternative — only promoting from within — can produce 'organizational incest' as exemplified by the stereotyped models of the good 'company man' or 'company woman' found in some banks and government departments. Organizations need new blood; bringing in outsiders is one way of achieving that (Hunt 1986, p.211).

3. Marketing

We will refer to this again in dealing with selection procedures but it is worth remembering that 'word of mouth' and informal communication are powerful influences. Applicants who have de-selected themselves and, more significantly, those **not** selected at interview will carry an image of the school or college to communicate to others.

Key learning points

- Recruitment is best seen as part of a continuous process involving selection and induction.
- Recruitment has a significant cost implication. Recruitment needs to be seen in as wide a context as possible to enable it to play its part in an organization's future, including implications for its future culture and structure.
- Recruitment, like selection, is affected by personnel legislation, particularly in relation to its formal procedures.

8. Selection

Introduction

In this section, we identify the issues involved in managing the selection of professional and support staff in educational organizations and examine the application of these issues in a study of selection processes. We also try to draw out principles underpinning selection management.

Study focus

At the end of this section, you should be able to:

- understand the difficulties involved in managing a selection process;
- identify key principles involved in managing all the elements of selection management;
- formulate proposals for the selection process which address the difficulties and apply the principles.

Issues in staff selection

For the manager of human resources, we suggest there are four issues which need to be addressed in managing staff selection.

❑ Linkage with recruitment and induction

The whole process which begins from the moment a potential vacancy is identified is best managed as a continuous one. Selection processes will be managed within the context of an organization's recruitment policy (see pp.49) and induction will be most effective if it is planned to begin the moment an appointment is confirmed. An example of the former is that the general procedures for appointing staff will be delineated when a recruitment policy is established. For example, a recruitment policy which refers to treating all applicants 'professionally' is placing a responsibility on its selection procedures to ensure that the actual mechanics (e.g. interview environment, lunch arrangements, time allocation) are efficiently organized, and that all candidates are entitled to a de-briefing.

❑ Acknowledgement of technical and functional aspects of the roles of staff

By this we mean that the selection has to recognize that it is concerned with:

- **what** an organization does; and
- **how** it does it.

An organization will succeed through the knowledge, abilities and skills of those who work in it ('technical' aspects) and the degrees of commitment, motivation and effort with which they apply these attributes ('functional' aspects). The latter are clearly affected by the character and personality of the individual and the culture and structure of the organization. If both these aspects have to be considered in managing the selection processes, the key question for the organization's managers is the extent to which both the technical and functional aspects of roles can be determined or assessed.

(a) Technical aspects

These are more easily assessed since, for example, the qualifications of candidates will inevitably be based upon knowledge and skills required to obtain them e.g. through examinations. There are also well established tests of abilities which can be used (although the key choice for selection managers may lie in determining **which** tests are appropriate for which abilities). This question of 'selection instruments' will be dealt with later.

(b) Functional aspects

The question of assessing the functional aspects of a person, however, is far more complex. It involves judgements about whether the person will 'fit in', their ability to work well in a team or the factors which will motivate them as individuals. Does, for example, the person share the values of the organization, not merely **say** so?

◉ Reading 11

Marianne Coleman and Tony Bush *Managing with Teams* Chapter 13.

Please read the first part of this chapter, up to but not including 'Team leadership'. Please pay particular attention to the section on 'Team Roles'.

Our comments

Belbin's work (Belbin, 1981) offers a clear example of why selection processes need to address the individual candidate's ability to contribute to the team or teams in the organization to which they will belong. If the best candidate in terms of technical aspects is a 'shaper' according to Belbin's typology, and the team already has a significant number of shapers, Belbin's research suggests that the team's performance may lack the commitment to accomplish very much.

Activity 8.1 (A) (R)

Analyse a team of up to 8 people of which you are a member in your organization, according to Belbin's typology. What balance of roles already exists? What is missing?

Please consider these questions in relation to the **technical** aspects of two posts which might occur in your school or college:

- teacher of a specific subject; and
- support assistant for AVA (Audio-Visual Aids)

Then consider the kind of characteristics relating to the **functional** aspects of a team role you would want to be addressed in selecting the best teacher or support staff member for the post.

Our comments

You may well have encountered some of the problems in applying this type of analysis. Not everybody fits the descriptors, or they do so only in certain circumstances. Others may act according to the micropolitics of the situation, and some people have inconsistent behaviour patterns.

The choice of selection instruments, therefore, and the manner of the management of the whole selection process both have a critical influence on its effectiveness and its outcome. By 'manner', we mean the methodology and the rationale of the selection process.

❏ The need for objectivity in a potentially very subjective process

Although it is tempting to assume that any subjectivity is bound to be related to functional aspects of the applicant's role (i.e. to their personality), it can easily be found in a failure to be objective about technical aspects. For example, one selector may be in favour of one candidate because he or she has a particular qualification rather than another. Alternatively, too much weight may be given altogether to academic achievement at the expense of other qualities which might be more relevant to effective performance of the job.

The need to bring objectivity to selection management touches upon important areas regarding selection personnel:

- Who should be involved in the process?
- Is training of selectors essential or desirable?
- If training is needed, what skills are required?

Managers will need to assess how helpful is the involvement of lay personnel, such as governors. In self-managing schools and colleges it is common practice for governors, for example, to be involved in staff selection — by statute. Research into the first grant-maintained schools in England and Wales found that governors exerted a powerful influence in this area (Bush et al., 1993). However, it can also be argued that professional managers need training in selection just as much as lay selectors.

If we examine some of the traditional practices which can distort a selection process, it is possible to identify a strong element of subjectivity. These practices include:

- basing judgements upon intuition rather than facts
- making 'snap' judgements
- insisting on a personal stereotype of what is a 'good' candidate
- comparing candidates with the previous post holder or with other candidates rather than the agreed criteria
- preferring a candidate in one's own image

Selection interviews, for example, have been demonstrated to be unreliable as predictors of performance by psychologists and researchers since the 1920s. Empirical work by Riches (1983) and Morgan et al. (1985) chronicles the use of poor selection interview techniques in education.

Thomson (1993) summarizes the shortcomings as:

- Interviewers often make up their minds about a candidate within the first five minutes of the interview and — consciously or unconsciously — spend the rest of the interview trying to justify their judgement.
- Interviewers' judgements of candidates can be affected by their appearance, speech, gender and race either positively or negatively; people tend to favour others whom they perceive to be like themselves.
- Few interviewers have undertaken any training in interview skills.
- Research on memory shows that we remember information we hear at the beginning and end of an interview and, thus, tend to forget vital details and facts given in the middle.
- It is impossible for the human brain to concentrate at the same level over a prolonged period; thus if you are interviewing several candidates on the same day, they may not receive equal amounts of your attention.
- Finally, the British Psychological Society has found that even well-conducted interviews are only 25 per cent better than choosing someone by sticking a pin in a list of candidates! (Thomson 1993, p.30).

It is noteworthy that the above list refers not only to individual prejudices that may occur but also to human factors such as memory and concentration.

Hackett (1992) notes some of the common forms of unconscious intuitive responses as:

a) The Halo Effect
This occurs where one feature of the interviewee becomes an over-riding factor which governs our perception of the person. A common pitfall is to assume that someone who is attractive and articulate is also intelligent.

b) Prejudice/bias

We tend to pre-judge people, either favourably or unfavourably, because they belong to a particular group or remind us of a particular person. Common prejudices include the assumption that members of one race are more hard-working than those of another, or that women are less reliable than men. These preconceptions will colour our interpretation of any comments they make.

c) Stereotypes

These take two forms:

(i) Good worker stereotypes. We may build up a picture in our minds of what a good worker is like, and then use the interview as a means of finding someone who matches that rather than the personnel specification. We will be favourably disposed to those who appear to match, and will be more critical of those who do not match. The most common stereotypes of the good worker are the 'boy scout' [sic] stereotype (who is a do-gooder and pillar of the community), and the 'human relations' stereotype (who is a jolly good chap [sic] whom everybody likes). Neither may be right for the job.

(ii) Physical trait stereotypes. We may identify one physical characteristic and assume that everyone who posesses that trait will be alike in character. Examples are the assumption that people with red hair have quick tempers and that people whose eyes are close together are not to be trusted. These unfounded assumptions will again colour our judgement and make it more difficult for us to evaluate information in a well-balanced way.

d) Unfavourable information

Most of us are more heavily influenced by people's bad points than by their good ones. Once we have formulated an adverse impression we are slow to change our minds (Hackett 1992, p.70).

All these elements of subjectivity indicate the critical need for selection to be managed as objectively as possible. Any process involving humans can never be completely free from some of the above elements, but they can be recognized as such and nullified as much as possible by informed management of the process. (See, for example Marianne Coleman, *Women in Educational Management*, Chapter 9).

❑ Equal opportunities

As we stated in **Recruitment**, legislation will need to be taken account of in:

- advertising;
- job description; and
- person specification.

Similarly, all parts of the selection procedure have to be managed to be sure no candidate is disadvantaged because of race, religion, gender or disability by, for example, requiring application letters to be hand-written which might discriminate against certain disabled candidates. Equally, it is arguable that a test of physical strength for a caretaking post involving portering would discriminate against female candidates. You might like to consider these and other similar questions to help you formulate ways of ensuring equal opportunities are provided throughout the selection process management.

Activity 8.2 (R)

Devise a method of checking all stages of the recruitment and selection processes to ensure that:

(i) No candidate will be discriminated against
(ii) Prejudices of selectors will be minimized

For example, you might devise a check-list of certain criteria against which all procedures are assessed. You may find it helpful to imagine specific scenarios, e.g. an interview candidate who is pregnant, and see if your check-list would hold good.

Our comments

Your success will depend on the extent to which the equal opportunities policy of your organization has encouraged you to develop positive attitudes and awareness. Remember that those in the outside world see selection as their first contact with the policies of the school or college. The policy areas listed by Armstrong in our section **HRM in Education** (p.18) offer a useful taxonomy of the policy areas that now need to be considered at school or college level.

Managing the process of selection

We suggest that the key issues to be considering in the management of selection processes are:

1. Personnel, i.e. **who** shall be involved in the process?

2. Criteria, i.e. **against which standards** shall candidates be assessed?

3. Weighting, i.e. the **relative** importance of the different criteria.

4. Instruments, i.e. **how** shall the candidates' performance be assessed?

5. Matching, i.e. **deciding** on which person is best suited to the post.

Most writers on staff selection procedures (e.g. Day et al., 1985; Bell, 1988; Southworth, 1990) adopt what might be called the traditional approach (i.e. application, reference, shortlist, interview) while stressing the need to manage the process as professionally as possible.

Selection is best viewed as a two-way process i.e. one that places equal emphasis on allowing candidates to determine that a post is suitable for them and on the organization being able to select the most appropriate person. An organization which, for example, puts pressure to accept an offer on the person whom it sees as the most suitable, when that person has significant doubts, runs the risk of appointing someone who may quickly become demotivated.

We now consider each of the five key issues identified above.

❑ 1. Personnel
The actual involvement of personnel may be determined through an organization's selection policy or by the selection procedures normally followed. A head of department or curriculum area may, for example, automatically be involved when the vacancy is in their own area. Equally, deputy heads or vice-principals may be involved for some or all of the process, whilst middle managers may be included in order to gain experience of selection and become proficient in it.

As mentioned earlier, the involvement of lay personnel such as governors may be mandatory but, in any case, the appropriate criteria for participation are the particular perspectives that the personnel involved may bring to the process. The involvement of lay personnel can often bring a valuable, different perspective from that of the professionals working within the organization.

Finally, the issue of training for those involved in selection needs to be considered.

❑ 2. and 3. Criteria and weighting
Criteria for selection may include:

biographical data such as qualifications and experience
skills technical, managerial etc.

knowledge e.g. of current legislation, health and safety, curriculum requirements

attitudes and values e.g. personal ambition, loyalty

others such as interests

It is in the weighting of the relative importance of the various criteria that the analysis of the job requirements will bear fruit. Bringing together the job description and person specification enables the drawing up of a check-list of selection criteria for all selectors to use **consistently**. Bell (1988) offers the following fictitious example of a weighted criteria check-list (Figure 8.1).

Teacher with special responsibility for mathematics	Importance weighting	Mr Brown		Mrs Green		Miss Lilac		Mr White	
		Actual score	Weighted score	Actual score	Weighted score	Actual score	Weighted score	Actual score	Weighted score
Teaching certificate	2	1	2	0	0	0	0	0	0
B.Ed. or similar	5	0	0	2	10	1	5	0	0
PGCE	4	0	0	0	0	0	0	0	0
Higher degree	2	0	0	0	0	0	0	2	4
Other advanced INSET courses	3	1	3	2	6		3	3	9
		Sub-total	5	Sub-total	16	Sub-total	8	Sub-total	13
Experience									
Infant	3	0	0	1	3	1	3	0	0
Junior	4	1	4	1	4	0	0	1	4
Other	1	0	0	0	0	2	2 (Special)	0	0
Curriculum change in maths	2	1	2	2	4	0	0	0	0
Co-ordinating work of colleagues	3	2	6	4	12	3	9	1	3
Providing school-based INSET	3	1	3	2	6	1	3	1	3
		Sub-total	15	Sub-total	29	Sub-total	17	Sub-total	10

Figure 8.1 Interview analysis sheet (Bell 1988, p.109)

Activity 8.3 (A)

Devise a criteria check-list — with weightings for use by selectors in appointing:

a) A deputy head or vice-principal of your organization.

b) A classroom teaching post.

c) A secretarial or clerical assistant post.

Our comments

You will probably have found the devising of weightings to be difficult because of the need to rank elements of the work — it is easy to say that one task is more important than another but rather more difficult to give it a value. However, this is one way in which we can overcome some of the inconsistencies in the selection process.

❏ 4. Instruments

'Instruments' are those devices or tools used in structuring the selection process. In that sense, some have already been referred to, such as job descriptions and application forms. We will confine ourselves here to four of the most important:

- interviews;
- tests;
- exercises; and
- assessment centres.

(i) Interviews

We suggest that the effective management of interviewing acknowledges the following key principles:

Interviewing is a two-way process. Since candidates can be appointed only on the basis on past performance and potential for future performance, it is important that they have the opportunity to relate their performance to date to the proposed job by, for example, being enabled to concentrate during the interview on describing past life and experience which is relevant to what is needed for the post available (Bolton, 1983).

Consistency in approach by interviewers. This has management implications for choice of personnel involved, training of interviewers, and a clear organizational policy on selection.

Interviewing involves specific skills. Since face-to-face interviewing is obviously a communication process, the skills involved are primarily those of communication.

◎ Reading 12

Colin Riches *Communication* Chapter 12.

Please now read the sections 'Barriers to Communication' and 'Communication Skills'. Relate the points discussed to personal experiences you have had both as interviewee and interviewer. Then proceed to the activity.

Activity 8.4 (A) (R)

Draw on your understanding of Riches, this text and your own experience to devise a handout of practical advice for interviewers, to be used at an actual interview or a training session for them. The handout should consist of a number of simple statements such as 'Do's' and 'Don'ts'. How far does your guide help with the framing of questions?

Our comments

Although we may become adept at the use of questions they may not elicit all that we need to know about candidates. Clearly, a vital skill for interviewers is that of questioning (Southworth, 1990). In everyday communication, questions are often used to obtain knowledge, but in a selection process the knowledge that an applicant has can be more easily ascertained through instruments such as written processes or exercises. Questions at interview should perhaps be 'concerned more with what [the candidates] have learned from experience and with their particular skills and qualities than with mere knowledge' (Day et al. 1985, p.68). Since the purpose of an interview is to be able to select the best candidate from candidates **at their best**, Southworth's definition of effective questions seems a useful summary.

A good question is one that encourages the interviewee to answer freely and honestly. A bad question is one that inhibits the interviewee from answering freely or produces distorted information (Southworth, 1990, p.134).

You may find it useful at this point to look at the handout you devised for interviewers. Does it help them in framing their questions?

Interviewing, however, is only part of the selection process. Historically, interviews have been seen as by far the most important part of the process and, in some cases, **all** important. Remembering the inadequacies of interviews, the inevitable risk is that the person appointed may be the person who performs best at interview, not the person who will perform best in the job, although statistically these will sometimes be the same person. In managing selection processes, therefore, we suggest it is important to have an idea of the **relative** importance (or weighting) of the interview, compared with other evidence upon which the assessment for selection will be based e.g. application letter, reference(s), informal discussion, exercises etc.

(ii) Tests

Psychometric tests (which can include work sampling, tests of ability or of personality) can be more reliable than interviews as long as two important conditions are fulfilled; first, that the test is relevant to the job and, secondly, that the people using the test are trained in its use.

In education, psychometric tests have not been widely used in the past but their use is growing. Technical ability tests are increasingly being used in appointments of technical support staff, for example. In the appointment of senior managers, personality diagnostic tests such as those based on Belbin's work, for example, are used to ascertain the suitability of leaders or potential leaders for working with others. In Great Britain in 1989, about 5 per cent of job applicants were given some kind of test, although the percentage was higher in sales jobs and in the transport industry, and lower in education (Smith et al., 1989).

Our brief extract below comes from a much fuller actual, but for obvious reasons anonymous, report on a candidate for a senior post in the educational world:

> Strengths: Strong on critical thinking and objectivity, scoring in the top percentile for verbal reasoning.

> Weaknesses: May be hypercritical and seen as intense by others, who may not be inspired by his/her level of drive and management style.

(iii) Exercises

The use of exercises of various kinds is developing in the educational world and examples include:

In-tray exercise. Candidates are asked to sift and prioritize and decide action upon a sample of documents.

Written report. Having been given certain information, candidates are asked to write a report for a particular audience.

Role play simulation. Candidates are asked to enact the job applied for in a particular situation.

Oral presentation. Candidates are asked to present formally to the interviewers a brief (usually 5 or 10 minutes) synthesis of their views or approach to a particular issue. Usually, candidates may use visual aids in support of their oral presentation e.g. slides or overhead projections.

Leaderless group discussion. Candidates are grouped together to discuss a topic or reach a decision on a question. Selectors are involved only as observers of individuals' performances with the group's processes.

Situations in which the groups are placed are usually co-operative (e.g. the group must come to a consensus on an issue), but operate within a competitive framework.

(iv) Assessment Centres

An assessment centre is a variety of testing techniques designed to allow candidates to demonstrate, *under standardized conditions*, the skills and abilities most essential for success in a given job (Joiner 1989, p.182) [our emphasis].

Joiner claims that good assessment centres 'can greatly improve a selection or promotional process particularly for jobs requiring a variety of skills in a variety of situational contexts' (p.173). Most people would recognize that teaching, for example, fits the job described here!

The centres therefore involve a series of individual and group exercises, observed by trained assessors. All the exercises are set within a common frame of reference (e.g. a set of stated criteria as to suitability for headship), and focus on assessing potential for success at a higher level than the assessee's current job demands.

In summarizing the whole issue of instruments available to managers of the selection process, we need to stress again that selection is a person-to-person process and therefore subject to human fallibility. Technical assessment methods are becoming more available and offer scope for greater impartiality, yet the culture and ethos of a particular organization confirms the necessity for that organization's representatives to be involved on a personal level via, for example, interviewing.

Morgan (1989) uses the phrase 'black box' to describe the criteria in the process which selectors use but have not explicitly agreed. He concludes that the challenge in managing selection processes is:

> how to accommodate requirements which can appear conflicting: the management need for impartial technical assessment methods to gather evidence on candidate fitness for headship; and the need to satisfy the demand for a visible democratic accountability and social legitimation by the local community. The application of the management perspective to selection in other public services has resolved this 'conflict' by ensuring that only those candidates who have satisfied the most rigorous technical assessment and are found to be capable of doing the job to a satisfactory minimum level of performance are offered to the 'democratic controllers' for appointment decision (Morgan 1989, p.169).

❑ 5. Matching

Finally, we come to the stage in the selection process of making a decision about which candidate best matches the requirements of the job. Here the selectors are **assessing** the **performance** of the candidates, through the **instruments** used. At this stage, the selectors will need to assess the **evidence** that has been derived from the instruments.

Morgan (1981) and Southworth (1990) have stressed the importance of applying the following notions to the evidence:

- Adequacy (how sufficient is it?);
- Integrity (how truthful and accurate is it?); and
- Appropriateness (how relevant is it?)

These are reproduced in the model in Figure 8.2

Norris (1992) offers the following model (Figure 8.3) of a 'Fair and Valid Selection Process'. This places the interview as central to the process while advocating the use of systematically managed approaches and technical instruments as appropriate.

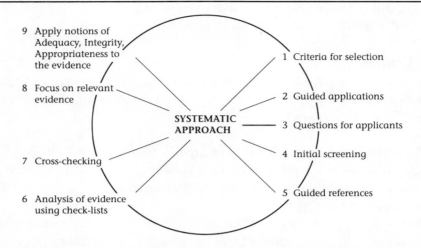

Figure 8.2 A systematic approach to analysing evidence (Southworth 1990, p.117)

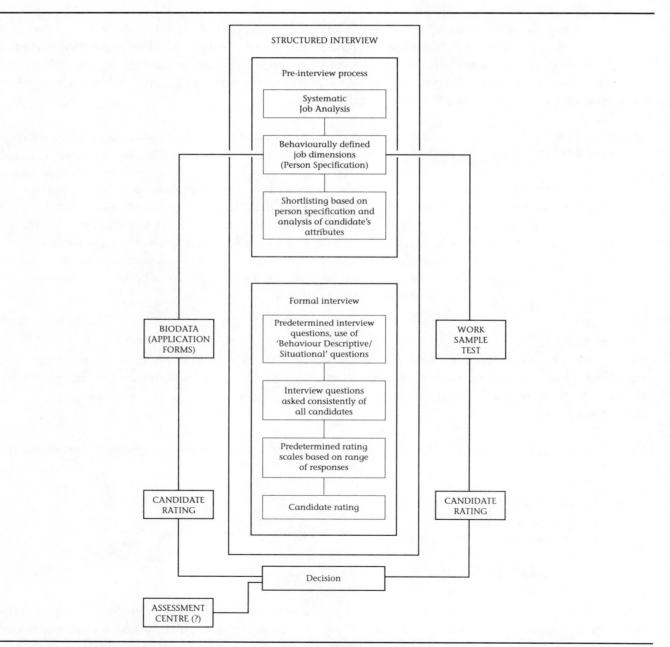

Figure 8.3 Model of a fair and valid selection process (Norris 1992, p.8)

Activity 8.5 (A) (R)

To finish the section on managing the selection process, we suggest you now draw up a model for use in your organization or one in which you hope to manage. Devise the model as a programme in **chronological** sequence, indicating action required at each stage. We suggest you begin:

(i)   **A vacancy occurs**
- Inform staff. How?
- Interview person leaving.
- Inform others. Who?
- Decide on selectors. How?

(ii) etc.

Make a marginal note at each stage where there could be a tension between personnel and human resource approaches.

Our comments

However good the selection process has been the new colleague has to be helped to understand the practice and culture of the organization and be offered opportunities for further development. In this sense recruitment and selection are the first two elements of a staff management process which also includes induction, mentoring and appraisal. The relevant issues relate to our discussions in **People or Performance** and **Individual and Organizational Development**. We now continue the application of those issues in the sections which follow.

Key learning points

- Selection is best seen as a continuous process involving recruitment and induction;
- Awareness of potential human prejudice is necessary to ensure the selection process is valid;
- A variety of selection 'instruments' exist which need to be carefully appraised and utilized to make selection management valid.

9. Induction and mentoring

Introduction

In this section we examine two other key elements in the management of performance. These are:

- **induction:** the process of ensuring effective performance during the initial period following appointment of a person to a new post; and
- **mentoring:** the process through which a person is supported in the organization by someone allotted to fulfil that support role.

The two elements are linked because induction in schools and colleges should, we propose, involve the new post holder being supported by a mentor. However, mentoring as a process has far wider implications than merely being used in the induction context.

Study focus

> By the end of this section, you should be able to:
>
> - understand the purpose of induction;
> - understand the importance of induction for all new post-holders;
> - examine the role of the mentor in induction;
> - understand the place of mentoring in the organization's development programme;
> - analyse what skills are involved in mentoring;
> - begin to devise effective induction programmes and mentoring policies.

Induction

Induction is essentially an initiation into the job and the organization. In the case of newly qualified personnel entering their first posts, it is clearly also an initiation into the profession.

Newly qualified teachers (NQTs), for example, have always been seen as both needing and being entitled to a formal or semi-formal induction. In schools run by District or Local Authorities, requirements for such induction have often been drawn up by these Authorities. Autonomous schools and colleges are increasingly responsible for this themselves. In England and Wales, the statutory requirement for all newly qualified teachers to serve a 'probationary year' (in effect an induction period with assessment) was abolished in 1992, leaving schools to arrange their own induction.

It could be argued that schools and colleges have a moral responsibility to new entrants to the profession: to provide effective induction because of the implications for the education of pupils and students generally, and also because of the costs involved in initial training. In addition, the notion of effective induction and mentoring acquire an additional significance with the move towards school or college-based initial teacher training (ITT) which is discussed in **HRM in Education**.

We believe that any school or college committed to effective management of human resources needs to manage quality induction for all employees taking up new posts. However, it is true to say that more attention has been given to the induction of beginners (NQTs) than other new post-holders (e.g. Earley and Kinder, 1994). The School Management Task Force (DES, 1990) recommended that in England and Wales a programme of induction for senior management be one of the key issues in implementing its recommendations for management development. The focus on senior staff was primarily an acknowledgement that induction for all new post-holders was not possible to achieve quickly and the process should therefore begin 'at the top'.

Purposes of induction

It is possible to identify three major purposes of induction in schools and colleges. These are:

- socialization;
- achieving competence; and
- exposure to institutional culture.

❑ Socialization

The so called 'socialization' of inductees is perhaps the most important issue in induction in effective organizations. Schein (1978) identified five elements in this process:

1. Accepting the reality of the organization (i.e. the constraints governing individual behaviour).

2. Dealing with resistance to change (i.e. the problems involved in getting personal views and ideas accepted by others).

3. Learning how to work realistically in the new job, in terms of coping with too much or too little organization and too much or too little job definition (i.e. the amount of autonomy and feedback available).

4. Dealing with the boss and understanding the reward system (i.e. the amount of independence given and what the organization defines as high performance).

5. Locating one's place in the organization and developing an identity (i.e. understanding how an individual fits into the organization (Schein 1978, pp.36–37).

Two implications for managers arise from this. The first is that the influence, reactions and attitudes of peers, managers and other employees have a significant impact on the success or otherwise of the induction. Secondly, the performance of the new person, and thereby the performance of the organization, will be affected by the success of that induction.

❑ Achieving competence

In learning how to perform in the new post, Kakabadse et al. (1987) suggest that the inductee's cycle will have three stages:

1. **Getting used to the place**, i.e. overcoming the initial shock and immobilization of the new organization and job demands.

2. **Re-learning**, i.e. recognizing that new skills have to be learned or how learned skills have to be re-applied.

3. **Becoming effective**, i.e. consolidating one's position in the organization by applying new behaviours and skills or integrating newly formed attitudes with ones held from the past (Kakabadse et al. 1987, p.8).

❏ Exposure to institutional culture

Hunt (1986) argues that the most important facet of induction is the 'transfer of loyalties to the new organization' (p.213). The issue of loyalties is associated with the school's or college's culture and values and, as such, it will have been addressed in the management of the recruitment and selection process. Various writers in education (e.g. Southworth (1990), Bell (1988), Day et al. 1985), see induction as **part** of the appointment process. Bell, for example, suggests that 'the appointment process does not end when the successful candidate has accepted the post. The appointment is, in fact, the start of another process, that of induction' (p.121). Thus, the issue of identification with the values and culture of the school or college (see John O'Neill, *Organizational Structure and Culture*, Chapter 5) will have begun to be addressed during recruitment and appointment. For the successful candidate, the induction process begins immediately after accepting the post.

This aspect of induction is probably much less common, however, for support staff in schools and colleges. As Hughes (1985) remarks: 'Regrettably, for non-teaching staff this approach is rarely pursued. There is a dearth of provision ...' (p.175).

Similarly, induction is rarely provided for temporary or part-time staff: 'in the misguided belief that they will not care much about the organization and that they are just there to do the job' (Thomson 1993 p.110).

Activity 9.1 (R) (C)

Research tool: interview

You will find it useful at this stage to reflect on:

1. How you felt and how you were helped at the start of your first post;
2. How you felt and how you were helped at the start of your present post;
3. How your school or college inducts newly qualified staff.

You might be helped by using the Kakabadse et al. typology as a framework. To see how others feel about the same organization, interview two recently appointed full-time and part-time colleagues about their experience of induction.

Remember that interviewing requires certain skills — preparation, structured approaches, consistency in the treatment of interviewees, and the provision of opportunities for the interviewee to contribute. You may well require these skills in your assignment or dissertation fieldwork and so it might help to keep a note of the strengths and weaknesses of your interview style.

Our comments

In all probability you will find that the larger the organization the more varied the experience — a reflection of the way in which interpersonal relationships build up. There are, however, ways of overcoming this hit-and-miss approach. It is to these we now turn.

Managing effective induction

Induction may involve some or all of the following:

- preparatory visits to the school or college prior to starting;
- obtaining information about the school or college;

- identifying the needs of the inductee in order to plan to meet them;
- offering guidance and support over personal (e.g. family) issues related to taking up the new appointment;
- allocating a specific person (mentor) to support the person during induction; and, in larger institutions,
- arranging off-site programmes for all new employees together.

Schools and colleges need to make decisions about the management of induction which reflect their own values and priorities as organizations:

Socialization and cultural integration. The degree to which this should be part of any formal programme is debatable and is a sensitive area. Issues such as appropriate forms of dress, how people are addressed, and informal communications networks within the institution are less contentious and will also arise during the early period in the post.

How long should the induction last? Employment legislation in many countries means that all appointments are made on a probationary or trial basis, pending satisfactory performance. Schools and colleges need to decide whether the induction period should coincide with this or, alternatively, end naturally when the need for support is deemed to be no longer there.

Assessment. Linked with the above point is the issue of whether induction should involve assessment of performance or whether policy should specify that the two be kept separate.

Internal promotions. People who change posts within the same school or college may be considered to have a need for and entitlement to some form of induction. This form of induction may well differ from that provided for those new to the organization.

There are also particular issues with regard to teaching which affect the management of induction:

- teaching is essentially an autonomous job. However strong the support, the new person is 'on their own' and classes cannot be set aside while the inductee learns.
- there is insufficient time to offer support, especially 'on the job' support.
- mistakes made in teaching cannot be taken back and wiped out.

We suggested earlier that ensuring effective performance was a central issue for those managing induction. Kakabadse (1983) argues that performance is directly related to attitudes to learning, both of the new person and of those around them. Indeed, outside education, 'numerous studies have shown that the induction method affects both the rate of turnover in the first six months and the rate of integration' (Hunt 1986, p.213).

Activity 9.2 (A)

Devise an induction programme for:

a) a newly appointed middle manager;
b) a newly appointed support staff member.

Your programme should include aims and outcomes and address the need for evaluation of the programme.

Our comments

Your programme may well have followed a model pattern for development. For example, O'Neill (1994d, p.303) suggests that all professional development programmes should:

- acknowledge the professional as an adult learner
- begin from an analysis of the professional's own practice
- explicitly link learning and workplace environments
- promote shared reflection
- focus on thoughts and feelings in addition to actions
- integrate whole school and individual development
- establish learning objectives for the purposes of evaluation.

You will need to establish success criteria to measure your effectiveness in meeting your aims. You will also need to determine how you are going to get evidence for the evaluation process.

Mentoring

Professional mentorship is a twentieth century phenomenon, but it is based on a much older principle which maintains that for people to develop they need the support of others. We suggest that in terms of effective human resource management:

- The best context for growth is where a person is valued as an individual and as a colleague.
- Individuals do not develop in isolation — feedback is essential.
- Each step in development begins with a review of where a person is *now*.
- It is not a sign of weakness to ask for help. Indeed, a request for help is an indication of a healthy climate of trust and commitment to personal growth.
- 'Mutual learning' relationships in an educational organization are of benefit both to individuals and the schools and colleges in which they work. Elliott-Kemp and Rogers (1982) argue that the interdependence of staff in schools is essential to the attainment of organizational goals.

Given these principles, it can be argued that mentoring should play a crucial role in the support and development programme arranged by schools and colleges. We propose therefore to examine management issues such as the selection of mentors, their training, and their role.

Firstly, however, we need to consider what a mentor is and the value of mentoring.

The value of mentoring

… A mentor is someone, usually a work colleague at the same or a higher level than the individual, for whom he or she is responsible, to whom the individual can go to discuss work-related issues. There is a sense in which the mentoring relationship is similar to that of the 'master–pupil' relationship in medieval times; the pupil is learning from the mentor's experience and the mentor's role is to encourage and nurture his or her protege. Mentors can pass on practical insight derived from experience and can pick up on new ideas and attitudes. They can help their proteges to set themselves realistic expectations and steer them in the right direction as far as their career aspirations are concerned. It can, and should, be a mutually rewarding experience. Many people value being able to pass on what they know, particularly when this is appreciated and others benefit from their knowledge and experience (Thomson 1993, p.111).

Smith (1993) suggests that:

all teaching and non-teaching staff would benefit from an effective system of mentoring which provides work related guidance and support; therefore, mentoring should be seen as a whole school management concept (Smith 1993, p.2).

Smith also maintains that mentoring:

is developmental for both the individual and the whole organization encouraging a climate of support, teamwork and openness which may well lead to improvements in teacher morale, stress level and address some of the serious retention issues facing the profession (ibid. p.20).

However, the issue of institutionalized (Byrne, 1991) or compulsory mentoring, such as the programme for potential candidates for principalship in Singapore (Stott and Walker, 1992), is contentious. Ehrich (1994) points out some of the difficulties which may arise from institutionalized mentoring. Unwilling participation is highlighted as a potential problem and Ehrich recommends a programme which is 'not imposed on staff and, therefore, not likely to be perceived as threatening' (p.16).

Research on mentoring is taking place in 1994 in six English universities, funded by the Esmée Fairbairn Foundation, with the University of Leicester focusing on mentoring in relation to newly qualified teachers, middle managers and new headteachers. Management decisions about the extent and value of mentoring **within** a school or college, however, would seem to depend upon:

- the relationship of mentoring to the existing culture of the institution; and
- the form and content of the mentoring.

The role of the mentor

Kram's study (1983) found that mentors fulfil two broad functions:

- **career**, in which the mentor provides support in *professional* development areas (such as skills and knowledge acquisition, situational advice, professional ethics, job-related advice, etc.); and
- **'psychosocial'**, where support is in *social* areas (such as encouragement, general support, stimulation, 'sound-board' needs, discussion of problems, etc).

Finn (1993) suggests that the tasks undertaken by mentors might include those which:

- Assist the protege to establish realistic career goals;
- Act as a sounding board for the protege's ideas and concerns;
- Challenge the protege to face up to decisions and opportunities;
- Act as a resource for the protege to access learning opportunities;
- Pass on professional knowledge;
- Coach in-work skills (p.152).

One of the essential components in clarification of the mentor's role is an understanding that it does **not** involve formal assessment of the mentee's achievements. Evaluation of the individual's performance is the responsibility of the line manager. This crucial distinction between the roles of the mentor and the line manager as evaluator is shown in Table 9.1.

Both support and monitoring are essential in managing performance. Nevertheless, an effective mentoring system represents real investment in people and offers the potential for continued investment across the three key stages, ITT, NQT and Continuing Professional Development.

Clarity of the role of the mentor would seem to indicate the need for a 'mentoring contract' to establish the rules of the relationship between mentor and mentee. This would involve:

- clear objectives,
- development tasks,
- monitoring and reviewing the progress of the relationship.

Table 9.1 Distinction between mentor and line manager

	Mentoring	Evaluation
Who	Colleague/peer	Line manager/superior
Nature	Formative	Summative
Purpose	Facilitate development of new skills	Judge performance
Accountability and reporting	To mentee	To own superior
Decisions arising	Responsibility of mentee	Head of institution
Climate	Trusting to experiment and practice, including risk of failure	Tendency to accord with required practices
Data accumulated	Belong to mentee	Filed in personnel records
Agenda topics	Determined by mentee	May be negotiated but agreed within context of organization's requirements
Value judgement	Drawn out from mentee	Made by line manager
Role of partner	Negotiated with mentee	Determined according to line manager's role
Involvement	Togetherness/partnership	Supervisor/subordinate relationship
Communication	Two-way, questioning	Reporting, commenting etc.

(adapted from Middlewood 1992)

Activity 9.3 (C)

List the elements you would like to see in a mentoring contract for yourself. Relate your list to Finn's tasks on pp.72 and note and explain any omissions you have made.

Our comments

Whatever the mentoring arrangement, this is only one form of support. One of the principal aims of human resource management is that challenging targets should be established in all areas of organizational activity together with identification of the professional support which is needed. (See, for example, Colin Riches, *Motivation*, Chapter 11).

Selection of mentors

It is possible to identify appropriate profiles, in terms of skills, qualities and experience, of people who might make good mentors:

- People who have had a variety of work experience in schools and are up-to-date;
- Staff with a good reputation in the school;
- People who are willing to give time to others;

- Someone who is competent in the skills of mentoring which include counselling, coaching, networking and facilitating;
- Members of staff who recognize their own learning needs;
- People trained for the job (Finn 1993, p.152).

The key requirement is that mentors should be excellent role models (Hickcox and House, 1990) and that they should be educative mentors. These criteria, however, do not resolve the issue of whether a mentor should be superordinate or peer. In the case of new Heads or Principals the pattern adopted is inevitably that of a more experienced peer, from another school or college, since they have no role peer in their own institution. Similarly, Louis et al. (1983) found that new managers consistently ranked peers as being both the most helpful and the most readily available during settling-in periods at work.

Of equal significance is the way in which mentors are allocated to mentees. Ehrich's comment (see p.72) about institutionalized mentoring illustrates the potential dangers of a formalized universal system which almost inevitably produces mentors and mentees who will not be committed to, or satisfied with, their personal selection or allocation.

Little (1990) has pointed out that for those managers wishing to implement mentoring roles, the challenge lies in the unfamiliarity of the mentoring role to the teacher, the organization and, indeed, the profession.

The training of mentors

Central to the issue of training for mentoring is the identification of the attitudes and skills involved in the mentoring role.

❏ Attitudes

Effective mentoring assumes acceptance of the idea of partnership or critical friendships 'entered into voluntarily, based on a relationship between equals and rooted in a common task or shared concern' (Day et al. 1990, p.194).

These partnerships 'illuminate underlying principles and ideas in a way that allows teachers to understand and accommodate one another [...] and sometimes to challenge one another' (Little 1990, p.178).

The idea of contracting is also relevant. Egan's views are helpful in this respect:

- The agreement should be negotiated, not imposed, by the parties involved;
- The agreement should be clear to all involved parties. They should know what 'helping' is about;
- Some kind of oral or written commitment to the agreement should be obtained;
- The agreement should be reviewed as the parties progress and revised if necessary (adapted from Egan, 1982).

❏ Skills

Given the qualities that Finn suggests as being necessary for effective mentoring, it is clear that there are many skills which training may need to address. These are likely to include:

- Ability to share ideas, perceptions, understanding and values;
- Active listening;
- Clarifying ideas and perceptions;
- Focusing;
- Challenging (adapted from East Midlands Nine, 1992).

Acton et al. (1993) identify the following taxonomy. We feel that this list of skills embodies the management approach demanded by our original premise (p.4):

- Motivation
- Effective listening
- Effective observing
- Body language
- Reflexivity
- Giving and receiving constructive feedback
- Negotiation
- Problem solving
- Managing stress
- Using time effectively
- Target setting (Acton et al. 1993, p.70).

A number of the skills thus identified correspond with those needed by an effective appraiser. This highlights potential confusions concerning the relationship between mentoring and appraisal. When you have studied the section on **Appraisal**, you may wish to reflect on possible approaches to managing this relationship. Shea (1992) includes integration of mentoring and appraisal as a long-term aim in his model which has been adapted for use in education by West-Burnham (1993).

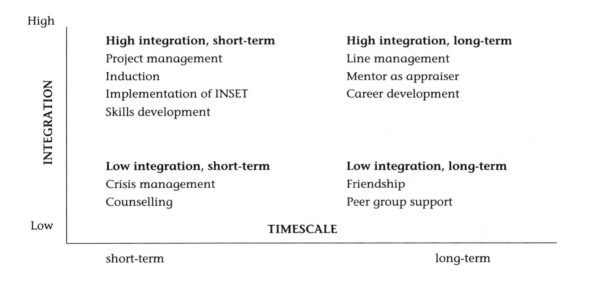

Figure 9.1 Mentoring relationships (West-Burnham 1993, p.132, adapted from Shea 1992, p.14)

West-Burnham argues that the model is useful because it emphasizes the importance of mentoring and appraisal as integral elements of the effective management of staff and:

> [...] it is argued that the integrated, long-term relationship is the norm for management development. However, integrated, short-term relationships will be appropriate for induction, preparation for a career change or to deal with a specific initiative (p.133).

Similarly, West-Burnham (1993, pp.133–138) argues that management development may be 'facilitated' through the use of mentoring techniques because mentoring involves reflective learning and networking within an institution and because it is 'not inconsistent' with a line management approach.

Key learning points

- Formal induction programmes address only some of the issues involved in integration of new employees;
- Mentoring is often linked with induction but can offer other benefits;
- Mentoring demands specific skills, distinct from those involved in line management or evaluation of performance;
- Implementing mentoring for all may have dangers as well as benefits; clarity of the mentor's role is the key factor.

10. Appraisal

Introduction

In education, the question of criteria for appraising performance is complex. In this section we wish to consider the **purposes** of appraisal, the management issues which arise and strategies for managing those issues. We then consider the components of an effective appraisal scheme and the special circumstances relating to appraisal in education. Finally, we look at managing the implementation and development of appraisal.

Study focus

At the end of this section you should be able to:

- understand the different kinds of approaches to appraisal and the possible tensions involved;
- describe the special issues involved in appraisal in education;
- identify the key elements in appraisal management;
- evaluate the relevance and validity of various teacher appraisal schemes;
- understand the **need** to address unsatisfactory performance in a constructive manner.

Managing optimum performance

Having managed the selection of the appropriate people and their induction into the job and the organization, it is vital to ensure that they perform to the best of their ability. We suggest that people work best when:

a) They know what is required of them
b) They receive guidance and support when necessary
c) They receive regular feedback on their performance

Education has not had a good record in providing feedback on performance. The professional autonomy of teachers in many countries and, indeed, the autonomy of schools and colleges has meant that decisions about promotion, for example, could be made on the basis of criteria unknown to anyone except the person conferring the promotion, including the fortunate recipient!

Clearly, in those cases, some form of 'appraisal' has taken place. Such practices, although less common in the 1990s, can still be described as: 'Closed systems [...] those where the boss assesses and records without discussion' (Hackett, 1992 p.98).

Activity 10.1 (R)

Before we undertake a detailed analysis of appraisal in education, it will be useful for you to reflect on the quality of feedback and support, both formal and informal, you have received in your career to date.

contd.

---

contd.

If you have worked in education for a number of years, you might ask yourself the following:

- How often have you been given **formal** feedback on how you are doing?
- When you last applied for a new post, did you know the contents of the reference written about you by your 'boss'?
- How have you known — **informally** — how well you have been progressing?

Whatever your period in education, the following questions are worth considering:

- Do I know the criteria upon which decisions about any promotions or additional salary increments are based in my organization?
- Do I know the extent of support I will receive if I apply for a post elsewhere?
- When was the last time someone senior to me observed me at work and discussed my performance with me?
- For informal feedback on my performance, **who** contributes to my awareness? Students? Colleagues? Parents of pupils?

Our comments

Your answers to these questions will provide a useful starting point as to how 'open' or 'closed' is the appraisal system in your current school or college. Our argument is that some form of appraisal takes place in all organizational activities, albeit under a number of guises. You may feel that a formal appraisal scheme would provide appropriate levels of support for your personal development. Equally, you may have experienced high quality support and feedback from colleagues outside any formal scheme, as part of your normal working relationships. In this section we encourage you to explore the relative merits and shortcomings of a variety of approaches to performance appraisal in education, and the management issues associated with each type of approach.

Purpose of appraisal

Here is one list of objectives of an appraisal system:

1. To provide a two-way boss–subordinate review of the subordinate's performance over the year

2. To feed back data to senior managers on the performance of an employee or a group of employees

3. To tell individuals what their strengths and weaknesses are

4. To provide data for reviewing salary and other rewards

5. To help with identifying training needs

6. To provide an inventory of talents, skills, qualifications, etc.

7. To provide input for human-resources planning, career-path planning and numerous other devices (adapted from Hunt 1986, p.222).

These objectives demonstrate that the mangement of appraisal schemes lies at the heart of the people or performance debate which we have already discussed in **People or performance**.

Some of the objectives above are concerned primarily with the purpose of **evaluation** of the individual's performance (1, 2, 4), some with the individual's **development** (3, 5) and some are mainly concerned with **accountability to the organization** (1, 2, 7). Clearly, some (1, 6) involve elements of more than one purpose. The question arises for managers as to whether the three purposes can be accommodated within one kind of appraisal system, whether different systems are needed for different purposes or, indeed, whether any of them require specific systems at all.

It might legitimately be argued that support for development requires trust and open dialogue, while evaluation requires information about areas for improvement or 'weaknesses'. Thus, there exists a potential conflict in appraisal between development and evaluation for control.

Beer (1986, cited in Fidler and Cooper 1988, p.6) separates the goals for these two areas.

1. Evaluation goals:
    a) to give feedback to subordinates so they know where they stand
    b) to develop valid data for pay and promotion decisions and to aid communication of these
    c) to provide a means of warning subordinates about unsatisfactory performance

2. Development goals:
    a) to counsel and coach subordinates so that they will improve their performance and develop future potential
    b) to develop commitment to the organization through discussion of career opportunities and career planning
    c) to motivate subordinates through recognition of achievements and support
    d) to strengthen supervisor–subordinate relations
    e) to diagnose individual and organizational problems

Beer summarizes the tension as it relates to appraisal for promotion.

> The individual desires to confirm a positive self-image and to obtain organizational rewards of promotion or pay. The organization wants individuals to be open to negative information about themselves so that they can improve their performance. As long as individuals see the appraisal process as having an important influence on their rewards (pay, recognition), their career (promotions and reputation), and their self image they will be reluctant to engage in the kind of open dialogue required for valid evaluation and personal development (Beer 1986, p.280).

To synthesize the management purposes in appraising performance, we can say that there needs to be:

a) Support for growth and development of the individual.

b) Evaluation of performance to identify:
    (i)   performance meriting reward
    (ii) performance requiring remedial action
    (iii) performance that is so unsatisfactory it requires termination of employment

c) Information concerning individuals' and groups' performance and needs to enable the organization to plan ahead.

Activity 10.2 (A)

List the ways in which your own organization offers 'reward' to its **'workers'**.

Sub-divide these into 'formal' and 'informal'. Against each one write down the criteria upon which you understand the merit reward to be based. Table 10.1 shows an example of this.

Table 10.1 Analysis by one teacher in a secondary school in London

Performance	Reward	Type	Criteria
'Good' exam results with taught class	'General' praise at departmental meeting by HOD	Informal	Pass rate of department higher than other similar departments
Standard of dress in tutor group 'good'	Personal praise from Pastoral Head	Informal	Fewer 'problem' referrals to Pastoral Head than other tutors
Organization of successful field studies visit	Commitment (written) to record in reference supporting application	Formal	No complaints received by HOD from pupils, parents or colleagues!
Being Stage Manager in successful school drama production	Mention in Principal's speech and newsletter!	Informal	Willingness to give up time for extra-curricular activity
Work on rationalizing assessment sheets in department	Given responsibility (unpaid) for Assessment Procedures in department	Formal	Careful and conscientious work to produce *useful* outcome

Our comments

You might find it helpful to expand your analysis by considering the following questions:

- Are there inconsistencies in the application of formal rewards?
- Do these relate to the criteria?
- How important is consistency here?
- Is it fair to include extra-curricular activities?
- Are the criteria in the formal situations explicit or implicit?

Now try a similar analysis relating to 'performance requiring remedial action'. You may find the analysis easier or more difficult. Whichever it is, does this give any indication of the emphasis in your own organization or unit?

Strategies for managing these issues

Clearly, strategies need to be employed that attempt to diminish the tension between evaluation and development highlighted by Beer (*op. cit.*). Strategies might include:

(i) Separating evaluation and developmental schemes.

A number of organizations outside education operate two distinct schemes. One is for personal development, the other is concerned with pay and promotion. You may wish to consider whether this separation strategy is feasible in a school or college.

(ii) Universal appraisal, including upward and peer appraisal.

Ensuring that **everyone** in the organization is appraised, including perhaps the opportunity for people to appraise their managers, can encourage a confidence in the system, a feeling of 'fair play'. It may also offer managers the opportunity to discover how their own performance is received. In schools and colleges, this approach assumes appraisal of the principal or headteacher, the person ultimately responsible for managing the appraisal system.

(iii) Recognizing that different systems may be needed for different groups of people.

The principal or headteacher is perhaps a special category. For example, the use of external perspectives (e.g. parents, governing bodies, inspectors) may be appropriate. Equally, it is arguable that vice-principals or deputy headteachers should manage the process.

Activity 10.3 (R) (C)

Consider the following description of what Hewton and West (1992, p.126) consider to be involved in effective headship:

> ... headship is centrally concerned with the identification and exploration of alternatives. This needs [...] the forms and functions of connoisseurship and the capacity to engage in educational criticism. [...] These could well be called the arts of headship, for headship is centrally concerned with disclosing the qualities of educational life in a language that is understandable to a range of stakeholders.

What special difficulties do you envisage in devising and developing an appraisal scheme for heads whose effectiveness will be judged in the above terms?

Our comments

The difficulties of developing effective appraisal for any kind of leadership post are related to the high degree of subjectivity in assessment of some of the competences involved. However, the work of Assessment Centres (p.63) is attempting to give more precision to this process.

Should all those who work in schools and colleges have the same scheme or should there be different schemes for, say, technical and administrative staff?

Components of appraisal systems

While schemes vary considerably, whether they be evaluative or developmental, or a mixture of both, there is almost universal agreement that any appraisal will need to include the following:

a) **Some form of self-review** through which the appraisee makes judgements about his or her own performance. This can be verbal but can make use of an organization's standardized pro-forma. This pro-forma may be merely a set of prompt questions or a detailed check-list. It may also include the appraisee's own ideas for improving future performance.

b) **Some collection of data about the appraisee**. These can include both **quantitative** (e.g. attendance and punctuality records) and **qualitative** (e.g. views of other people affected by the appraisee's performance) data. Sensitive management issues here concern appropriate sources of information, the type and detail of information sought, and the need to avoid 'gossip'.

c) **Observation of the appraisee at work**. It would seem foolish to envisage appraising someone's performance without actually **seeing** them at work, but there are difficulties. The essentially passive nature of some activities (e.g. working at a keyboard) and the private nature of others (e.g. teaching) clearly affect the validity of conclusions drawn from any observation of them.

d) **Interview meeting between appraiser and appraisee**. This interview serves quite a different purpose from the selection interview we examined earlier. Here, three different types of interview can be identified (after Maier, 1976).

> In the **'Tell and Sell'** method, the manager directs the interview and gains the acceptance of the appraisee to take steps to improve performance. The **'Tell and Listen'** style requires the manager to give authentic feedback but then to allow the appraisee to respond. Communication and understanding may be much improved. Changes in performance, however, depend upon a change of attitude following improved communication. The **'Problem-Solving'** style as the name implies requires both appraiser and appraisee jointly to acknowledge problems and to work on them together (Fidler 1988, p.10).

e) **Targets being set**. In the introduction to this unit, we identified **Targets** under both 'Commitment' and 'Performance' as being one of the crucial elements in the effective management of human resources in educational organizations. Targets being set as part of an appraisal scheme are valuable because they are recognized by the organization and carry an explicit commitment to action related to them.

f) **Follow-up**. Unless action is taken to follow up issues identified through the appraisal, there can be no improvement in performance. Clearly, this has resource implications, both in financial and human terms. As far as appraisal of teachers is concerned, advice was given in various local education authorities in England and Wales, that a sum of money should be earmarked to meet outcomes of the appraisal process.

Special issues for appraisal in education

Six significant issues arise for the management of appraisal in educational organizations. We need to examine these carefully in considering how to appraise performance most effectively in schools and colleges.

Firstly, teaching is a very autonomous and individual task. No two teachers are the same: teaching is an occupation in which performance is affected very much by the individual nature and personality of the person concerned.

Secondly, teaching is a multi-task job. There are, therefore, particular difficulties in assessing the effectiveness of carrying it out.

Thirdly, education involves uncertainty over measurement of results. Outcomes are unclear and, furthermore, are dependent not upon the staff directly but upon the achievements of those for whom the organization exists i.e. the students, however those achievements are measured.

Fourthly, in education there are no clearly defined 'rewards' in the business sense.

Fifthly, there are no simple means of attributing the 'results' obtained by students to specific teacher performance. The concept of value-added measures of performance (see **People or performance**) remains controversial in education.

Sixthly, there are a considerable number of stakeholders in education and, even where a teacher has a line manager, there are a number of other people who have a direct interest in the teacher's performance. A teacher of a class of children in their first year of formal schooling, for example, will often feel as parents gather to collect their offspring that he or she has thirty 'bosses'!

Given these difficulties, all of which acknowledge that educational organizations are above all dependent 'for their success on the quality, commitment and performance of the people who work there' (p.4), we would agree with West-Burnham's (1992) assertion that appraisal should be primarily for GROWTH and DEVELOPMENT. The appraisal process, therefore, should be kept separate from procedures designed to address competence, grievance or discipline matters:

- remedial action deals with capability issues;
- sanctions deal with disciplinary matters;
- performance related pay deals with financial recognition of performance (adapted from West-Burnham 1992).

Prior to teacher appraisal being introduced in England and Wales, research projects and pilot studies strongly emphasized the need for positive approaches. In a summary of these studies, Montgomery and Hadfield (1989) found that:

- an emphasis on being positive and constructive in comments on teaching performance was critical to the success of appraisal.
- because a teacher's personality and self-image were so evident in classroom performance, any comments were inevitably construed as very personal in nature.
- a concentration on weaknesses rather than identified strengths simply led to hostility and negative reaction.

Activity 10.4 (A)

If appraisal is to have a positive approach, we suggest you will need to build this into all stages of the appraisal process.

1. Devise a self-review pro-forma which meets this criterion. Ask a colleague to complete the pro-forma. Discuss the outcomes with the colleague and revise the form if necessary.

2. Write out four targets for yourself in your own performance in your organization for the next twelve months. Then check:
    a) Do they contribute to the organization's development plan?
    b) How would someone else assess whether you had achieved them or not?
    c) Do they address any of the questions raised in your self-review pro-forma?

3. How do the six special issues for appraisal listed earlier (p.82) affect the evaluation of your targets?

Our comments

You will see that appraisal cannot be handled in isolation from the development of both the school or college and the individual teacher. Implementation of an appraisal scheme has to recognize these twin demands.

Managing the implementation and development of appraisal

Your appraisal scheme may well be operating within statutory requirements and certain institutional interpretations of guidelines. There may be a 'code of practice' in the institution. All these need to be carefully noted and incorporated into any system and its practice. We believe it is helpful for managers to be aware of the conditions under which appraisal is most likely to succeed, i.e. the features of the organizational culture in which it operates. Experience has indicated that these include:

- A consensus about values in the organization.
- A climate or ethos of trust and openness.
- An encouragement of access to self-development for people.
- An encouragement of a positive self-image amongst people.
- A prior agreement of what commitment will be given to supporting and achieving outcomes of appraisal.
- Job descriptions in which the job-holders have 'negotiated' the content.
- Appropriate preparation and training for participants.

The final point may be worth special consideration. Whereas the first five are aspects of organizational culture which can be affected gradually, training for appraisal is specific. We turn now to a discussion of the various approaches to the matching of appraisers with appraisees.

Matching appraisers with appraisees

There are different models of appraisal in this area. It has been argued that any educational organization:

> that does not use its management structure as the basis for appraisal relationships calls into question the role and functions of its so-called managers. (If managers [...] are not responsible for the development of their colleagues then they could be seen as overpaid classroom teachers and highly overpaid administrators) (West-Burnham 1994b, p.29).

Whoever are the appraisers, we would maintain that the **method** of choosing appraisers is critical to the success of the eventual match between appraiser and appraisee. Whichever method is used, it should be open, that is, publicly documented and consistently applied.

Methods for selection of appraisers include:

- The overall appraisal manager allocating appraisers.
- Allowing appraisees to choose either from a long list or limited list.
- Allowing appraisers to choose.
- Allowing 'negative preference' (which one(s) are *not* wanted).
- Drawing names out of a hat!
- Secret ballots.

Finally, let us address the most critical issue for management of appraisal in education — what form is the appraisal of the central educational tasks to take? One approach, widely used in the USA, for example, is through a list of competencies against which each teacher is 'measured'. Another approach involves the appraiser and appraisee negotiating and agreeing the areas of the teacher's work which shall be appraised.

Before we conclude this section by asking you to consider three case studies, it will be useful to summarize certain terms:

- *Teacher competency* refers to any single knowledge, skill or professional value position, which is relevant to successful teaching practice.
- *Teacher competence* refers to the repertoire of competences a teacher possesses. Overall competence is a matter of the degree to which a teacher has mastered a set of individual competences.
- *Teacher performance* refers to what the teacher does on the job rather than to what he or she can do. Teacher performance is specific to the job situation.
- *Teacher effectiveness* refers to the effect that a teacher's performance has on pupils. Effectiveness depends not only on competence and performance but also on the response pupils make.

Case studies

❑ Bob

Bob is a 28-year-old teacher at a High school in Georgia, USA. His supervisor appraises him using the Georgia State scheme of competencies and indicators. There are sixteen competencies and a total of fifty indicators. Fourteen of the competencies relate to performance in the classroom. For example, competency six is structured as shown in Table 10.2.

Table 10.2 Competency VI (uses instructional techniques, methods and media related to the objectives)

Indicator 1	Uses teaching methods appropriate for objectives, and learners and environment
Indicator 2	Uses instructional equipment and other instructional aids
Indicator 3	Uses instructional materials that provide learners with appropriate practice on objectives

The other two competencies relate to professional responsibilities and development, including indicators such as:

- Demonstrates ethical behaviour; and
- Participates in professional growth activities.

❑ Marguerite

Marguerite is a 34-year-old teacher in Ayrshire, Scotland. Her vice-principal appraises her classroom performance using the following 'appraisal instrument' (Table 10.3) which Cameron-Jones (1991) suggests is typical of those used in Scotland.

Table 10.3 Typical 'appraisal instrument' used in Scotland (Cameron-Jones 1991, p.48)

Focus		Target
1.	The teacher's knowledge of the subject	A sound knowledge and content was evident in every aspect/phase of the teaching.
2.	The way the teacher structured the information	The content was structured and sequenced appropriately for pupils, within and between the successive phases of teaching and learning.
3.	The way the teacher explained and presented the content	The explanations given were clear. Examples, illustrations and tasks presented to pupils were valid for the underlying principles/concepts of the content and for the skills to be learned by the pupils.
4.	The teacher's questioning and other elicitation of pupil responses	The elicitation methods used (verbal including questioning, and also non-verbal) were appropriate for the facilitation and progression of learning.
5.	The teacher's responsiveness and rapport with the pupils	The responses given to pupils' work/ideas/activities/selves were valid and encouraging.
6.	The way the teacher resourced the lesson	The resources for teaching, learning etc., were suitably deployed.
7.	The teacher's timing and pacing of the lesson	The timing and pacing of successive activities were positively responsive to the pace and nature of the pupils' learning.

Author index

Index

Feedback

EMDU is committed to providing the best learning resources for management development in schools and colleges. The authors would positively welcome your evaluation of the quality and relevance of the text and activities. Please feel freee to send any comments to John O'Neill, David Middlewood and Derek Glover at:

EMDU
School of Education,
Queen's Building,
Barrack Road,
Northampton
NN2 6AF
Facsimile: 0604 231136